Ideology and Politics On The Eve Of Restoration:

Newcastle's Advice To Charles II

Ideology and Politics
On The Eve Of Restoration:

Newcastle's Advice To Charles II

Transcribed and with an introduction by

Thomas P. Slaughter
Department of History, Rutgers University

The American Philosophical Society
Independence Square : Philadelphia
1984

Publication of this volume has been made possible by the
  John Louis Haney Fund.
Typesetting: The Historical Society of Pennsylvania
Printing: Port City Press, Inc.

Library of Congress Catalog Card No. 83-73278
International Standard Book Number: 0-87169-159-0
US ISSN: 0065-9738

To

Lawrence Stone

Contents

Acknowledgments

I thank the Bodleian Library, Oxford University for permission to publish this transcription of Newcastle's letter of advice. I am indebted to Professors Quentin Skinner of Cambridge University and John M. Murrin and Joseph R. Strayer of Princeton University, who read my introduction to the document, offered valuable advice, and supported its publication. I also thank Professors J.G.A. Pocock of Johns Hopkins and Joan Thirsk of Oxford University for their support.

Finally, and most of all, I stand deeply indebted to Professor Lawrence Stone of Princeton University. It was he who found the Newcastle letter in the Bodleian Library, secured a microfilm copy, and suggested that I undertake a study of its provenance as a project for his graduate seminar. His help at every stage of the process toward publication has been immense and inspiring. I knew well of the power of his mind as scholar before I met him, but have only since learned of his passionate dedication as a teacher. He has taught me much more than the history of England.

Acknowledgments

Introduction

Among the Clarendon papers held by the Bodleian Library at Oxford and also in the Portland Manuscripts at Welbeck Abbey appear copies of a long and detailed letter of advice written to Charles II on the eve of the Restoration. Until the twentieth century the "Advice" was attributed to Edward Hyde, Earl of Clarendon and Lord Chancellor during the early years of Charles's reign.[1] In 1903, however, Arthur Strong found that the handwriting of the Welbeck copy was identical to other documents written by William Cavendish, Earl of Newcastle.[2] Other evidence corroborates the essential correctness of Strong's claim.[3] The letter was apparently written by Newcastle in late 1658 or early 1659 and presented to Charles during the spring of 1659.[4]

Those few modern historians who cite the letter have minimized its significance as a historical document. David Ogg, among others, dismissed the political importance of Newcastle's advice. "It is at least certain," wrote Ogg, "that the counsels of the dissertation had no influence on royal policy; for its

---

[1] Falconer Madon attributed the fair copy held by the Bodleian to Clarendon. Madon, ed., *A Summary Catalogue of Western Manuscripts in the Bodleian Library at Oxford...*, 3 (Oxford, 1895): 567.

[2] Arthur Strong, ed., *A Catalogue of Letters and Other Historical Documents Exhibited in the Library at Welbeck* (London, 1903). Strong observed that three other items near the letter in the collection, one signed by Newcastle, are written in the same hand. Those include, according to Strong, "notes in the handwriting of the (first) Duke of Newcastle for the book on Horsemanship which he published in London, in 1667" (Strong, p. 53); "A Note for Andrewe Clayton about my Building att Welbeck" (pp. 56-57) that was signed "W. Newcastle;" and a "Book containing songs and sketches of plays in the handwriting of the D. of Newcastle" (p. 57).

[3] Margaret, Duchess of Newcastle, in her *Life of the Thrice Noble, High and Puissant Prince, William Cavendish, Duke, Marquess, and Earl of Newcastle* (London, 1667), mentioned that her husband, "when he was in banishment, presumed out of his duty and love to his gracious master, our new sovereign king, Charles the second, to write and send him a little book, or rather a letter, wherein he delivered his opinion concerning the government of his dominions, whensover God should be pleased to restore him to his throne."

[4] William Newcastle, Antwerp, to Secretary Nicholas, 18 April 1659, in C.H. Firth, ed., *The Life of William Cavendish, Duke of Newcastle* by Margaret, Duchess of Newcastle (London, 1886), 207. Madon, *Summary Catalogue (p. 54, n. 1)* mistakenly believed that the letter was written in 1660 or 1661. The fair copy of the letter itself clearly states that it was written and presented to Charles before his Restoration in 1660. Margaret Newcastle's *Life* (see n. 2) also noted that the letter was written during her husband's "banishment." Newcastle's letter to Secretary Nicholas in 1659 solicited presentation of a long letter, probably the one in question, to the king.

extreme length precludes the hope that Charles ever read it."[5]
Arthur Strong also argued that the advice did not have "any
effect upon the policy of Charles II."[6] Most historians of the
Restoration, however, have simply ignored the letter. No copy
of it has appeared in print since Strong's 1903 publication of
the Welbeck copy.[7] No edition of the fair copy held by the
Bodleian Library has ever before been published.

In reality, the direct political impact of the document can be
neither proved nor disproved. There exists no evidence that
Charles either read or did not read the letter. Only Secretary
Nicholas's assurance to Newcastle that the "Advice" was presented to the king survives. What can be established, however,
is that claims that Charles "did not take" Newcastle's advice are
misleading. In large measure, many actions in which Charles
engaged on his own initiative and that clearly represented his
personal preferences were remarkably similar to Newcastle's
vision of wise government.

Newcastle's letter represents also a political and philosophic
view of the world not uncommon or unimportant in Restoration England. At a time when virtually everyone felt insecure,
there were many men who noted similarities to a Hobbesian
type state of nature and who longed for return to the England
of Queen Elizabeth. Although times had changed dramatically
and the recrudescence of Cavalier spirit never restored the
halcyon days of the Elizabethans, some men lived who still
remembered nostalgically the years of the Virgin Queen. Both
Hobbes and Newcastle traced the troubles of their times to
fanaticism and decried how "the Bible in English under every
weaver's and chambermaid's arm hath done us much hurt."[8]
Both longed for the comparative tranquility of the past.

This, then, is the significance of Newcastle's advice. The
letter depicts a resurgent attachment to tradition that per-
vaded the thoughts of most members of the Restoration Parliament, of elder Cavaliers like Newcastle and Clarendon, the
aging political philospher Thomas Hobbes, the king himself,

---

[5] David Ogg, *England in the Reign of Charles II*, 1. (Oxford, 1924); 147.

[6] Strong, *Catalogue*, VII. A.C.A. Brett also mentioned the letter in *Charles II and His Court* (London, 1910), 154-156.

[7] Brief excerpts from the letter were published in Joan Thirsk, *The Restoration* (London, 1976), 3-4, 32, 115, 170, and 184.

[8] Draft of Newcastle's Advice," Strong, ed., *Catalogue*, 188. "Fair Copy," Bodleian Library Ref., Clarendon MS. 109.

and many who looked to the past for values and the security
that politics lacked under the later Stuarts. One might rea-
sonably argue that these men were largely out of step with
their times, that the future belonged not to Hobbes and the
Cavaliers, but to Harrington, Locke, and the Whigs. To dis-
miss them so lightly, however, ignores the very real impact of
their policies and the fact that they represented a significant
body of actors and thinkers within Restoration society. By
understanding how Newcastle came to think and write in
largely Hobbesian terms; why he would presume to foist such
views on the king; and why Charles, if not demonstrably re-
ceptive to the advice of this particular document, clearly
shared the world views of both Newcastle and Hobbes, we
come to know better the context of political action in Restoration England and the patterns of thought that shaped do-
mestic and international affairs.

*   *   *   *

Newcastle offered his "Advice" as one with "no oratory in it,
or anything stolen out of books for I seldom read anything,
but these discourses are out of my long experience to present
your majesty with truths that great monarchs seldom hear."[9]
He divided the letter into fifteen separate categories ranging
from suggestions about the militia, the Church, and the law; to
ceremony and order, "Your Majesty's Devertisements," the
governing of Scotland and Ireland, and the conduct of foreign
wars.[10] The length and detail of the letter preclude the possibility for summary here of the entire document.[11] I do wish
to offer a brief account of the advice, however, as an introduction to the document itself and as a basis for establishing
clearly the Hobbesian nature of the letter. Also of interest

---

[9] Ibid., "Fair Copy," 1. Not printed in Strong, ed., *Catalogue*.

[10] These categories included, in order of presentation, "For the Militia," "For the
Church," "For the Law," "For the Sivell Law," "For Trade," "For the Country," "For
Ceremony and Order," "Errors of State and their Remedies," "Of the Court Tables,"
"For Your Majesty's Devertisements," "For Country Recreations," "For the Govern-
ment of Scotland," "For the Government of Ireland," "For Government in General,"
"For Foreign States," and "For France and Spain."

[11] The letter is sixty pages long in Strong, ed., *Catalogue* and eighty-eight pages in the
fair copy.

are those portions of the letter that parallel actions taken by the first Restoration Parliament and by Charles on his own initiative and that reflect the king's personal preferences. Both the Hobbes connection and the actions of Charles will be discussed in greater detail elsewhere in this introduction.

Of primary concern to the monarch who wishes to rule England, according to Newcastle, must be control of the militia and of London. "Without an army in your own hands," he wrote, "you are but king on the courtesy of others. . . .Control London, master that city and you master the whole kingdom."[12] In order to subdue London, the king should grant the city a new charter that leaves all but military affairs in its hands. Charles should carefully attend to the politics of London, but "never violate any of their privileges for trade and they will remain loyal."[13] In the countryside, the king should keep the "traynde bands" (militia) active to subdue local insurrections and have only one lord lieutenant in each county, and the counties would remain calm and never again become ridden with faction. Close attention should be paid to the choosing of judges, sheriffs, and justices of the peace, but "the main business is a troup of horse in every county. . .to be paid from your own hand" for power remains the source of all authority. Not even the nobility are a "threat to the king as long as he keeps the force in his own hands."[14]

The successful ruler must also exert personal control over the Church. "Monarchy is the government in chief of the whole body politic," he wrote, "in all its parts and capacities by one person only. So that if either the whole body politic be under any pretence governed in chief by more than one generally it is no monarchy." If both the civil and ecclesiastical states "be not governed in chief by one and the same person, they cannot be said to be parts of the same monarchy." The king must "take control of the established church and remain on guard against Pope and Presbyterianism."[15] The former social positions of the bishops should be secured, lecturers strictly outlawed, and none but orthodox clergy and pupils permitted into the universities. There were already too many

---

[12] Strong, ed., *Catalogue,* p. 176.
[13] Ibid., 177.
[14] Ibid., 211.
[15] Ibid., 182.

scholars in the universities anyway. "Each university should have one half the number [of students and] they would be better fed and taught."[16]

Sermons throughout England should be tightly controlled, and here the Russian example was instructive.

> The emperor of Russia finding the people apt to commotions being stirred up by the pulpits, made a law that none should preach any sermons but what was delivered by the bishops to the ministers and printed and brought a great quiet and settlement to his kingdom only by this means.[17]

There should also be strict control of the printed word, "no disputation but in schools, nor no books of controversy writ but in Latin or else people get overheated with passion."[18] Newsletters circulating in manuscript, which had done great harm to the prestige of the government and Charles I, should also be ruthlessly suppressed. Economic exactions that annoyed the public and benefited only the clergy should, however, be relaxed. Ecclesiastical courts should be gentle to the laity and not excommunicate for every 'tithe sheafe' or be litigeous for that will never gain the people."[19] This last advice reflects the anti-clerical views of the Hobbesian circle.

Lawyers should also be curbed. Before the Reformation the Church had "swelled up so as to all but consume the kingdom." But after the Reformation, the law and lawyers had taken its place and the legal profession "grew to be so numerous and so vast a body as it swelled to be too big for the kingdom, and hath been no small means to foment and continue the Rebellion." Newcastle saw no real way to diminish lawyers' influence since they "have taken so deep root," but hoped that control of printing and drastic reduction of the numbers of students in universities and Inns of Court would help. "If you cut off much reading and writing, there must be fewer lawyers and clerks."[20] Even though great benefits would accrue to Charles by bringing the Church and the law under his personal control, Newcastle reemphasized his fundamen-

---

[16] Ibid., 188.
[17] Ibid., 187.
[18] Ibid., 189.
[19] Ibid., 190.
[20] Ibid., 192.

tal contention that nothing will nor can "confirm your majesty in a settled throne without your power, which is arms."[21]

In the matter of trade the Earl observed that "it is the merchant only who brings honey to the hive." If the king kept the merchants wealthy, controlled the Thames and London, made sure that exports exceeded imports, and never debased the coinage "trade and traffic [would] fill the kingdom with money."[22]

The "Advice" also enumerated major errors of the previous two reigns. The suggestion here again was that Elizabeth's reign represented a golden age of princely government. The greatest error of the Stuarts, according to Newcastle, was that

> they ever rewarded their enemies and neglected their friends . . . .[and they allowed their] subjects to dispute the king's per- ogative in Westminster Hall and in parliament to let everybody see what the king may do and what he may not do. Nothing makes a king cheaper or pulls him down more than this for it is an old maxim the king can do no wrong and it is most true for he is above the law and so are all governments.[23]

Appropriate regal behavior in these areas required a tighter control over the Privy Council among other remedies. The king must make sure that he had the best intelligence network in the kingdom. "He that has most and best intelligence must be wisest." "Do not hesitate to use money to buy intelligence . . . .Intelligence is the life of the state. . .and therefore noth- ing should be spared for intelligence."[24] Finally, and redun- dantly, the "Advice" argued that a king who "cannot punish and reward in just time cannot govern."[25]

In Newcastle's categorization of Stuart errors, Elizabeth's reign always provided the example for rectification. The queen did not call parliaments too often nor keep them very long in session. She was sparing in her creation of peers and never sold titles to the highest bidders. She neither permitted subjects to dispute her prerogative nor took advice from too large a group of counselors. Finally, and here Newcastle most longingly recalled the Elizabethan years, each class knew its

---

[21] Ibid., 201.
[22] Ibid., 203.
[23] Ibid., 217-218.
[24] Ibid., 220.
[25] Ibid., 221.

place during the queen's rule. Helpful in this regard would be a close attention to the maintenance of ceremony and order. "What is a king," Newcastle asked rhetorically,

> more than a subject but for ceremony and order [?] When that fails him he is ruined. . . .When you appear to show yourself gloriously to your people like a God, for the holy writ says we have called you Gods,—And when the people see you thus they will [get] down [on] their knees which is worship and pray for you with trembling fear and love as they did to Queen Elizabeth whose government is the best precedent for England's government absolutely, only these horrid times must make some little addition to set things straight and so to keep them.[26]

All of the passages summarized above have essential correspondences in either or both of Hobbes's treatises *Leviathan* and *Behemoth*. (Since *Behemoth* was not published until 1679, only *Leviathan* remains of concern here.) One is easily tempted, therefore, to assert a direct link between the two men. C.H. Firth, for one, did just that when he observed that "in his reflections on the past and his recommendations as to the future Newcastle echoes the views of Hobbes."[27] The ideas expressed in Newcastle's "Advice" circulated widely, however, among Englishmen during the mid-seventeenth century. Some of the notions expressed in the letter were, in certain respects, just as compatible with those of Gerrard Winstanley, an exponent of the radical left wing of Puritanism. Newcastle and Winstanley shared, for example, a passionate mistrust of learning derived solely from books. Talking and writing books, argued Winstanley, is "all nothing and must die; for action is the life of all, and if thou dost not act, thou dost nothing."[28] Similarly, if less passionately, Newcastle boasted in the preface to his "Advice" that he "seldom read anything" and elsewhere wrote that a future king should rather "study things than words, matter than language. . .for too much contemplation spoils action, and virtue consists in that."[29] Hobbes, too, is said to have bragged that he had read few works by other men.[30]

---

[26] Ibid., 210.

[27] Firth, ed., *Life of William Cavendish*, xxii.

[28] Quoted by Christopher Hill, *The World Turned Upside Down* (London, 1972), 386.

[29] Henry Ellis, *Original Letters Illustrative of English History*, first ser., 3 (London, 1825): 288.

[30] John Aubrey, *Brief Lives*, edited by A. Clark, 1 (Oxford, 1898): 349.

Most of Newcastle's advice lacks, however, the universality implied by such observations. The heart of his philosophy stands opposed to all theories, Winstanley's included, that emphasized the reason and equality of men above the ruthless competitiveness of human nature and the necessity for established hierarchy to maintain order. Both Hobbes and Newcastle emphasized that the basis of regal authority was power, that the important consideration was not who the sovereign was but whether or not he could maintain order among his subjects and retain his throne.

Hobbes argued as strongly as Newcastle that the ruler of a nation must control the militia.

> For the power by which the people are to be defended consists in their armies, and the strength of an army is the union of their strength under one command, which command the sovereign instituted therefore has; because the command of the *militia*, without other institution, makes him that has it sovereign. And therefore whosoever is made general of an army, he that has the sovereign power is always generalissimo.[31]

The philosopher also emphasized his belief that a large city like London, unrestrained, could wreak havoc on the authority of a sovereign. "Another infirmity of a commonwealth," Hobbes wrote in *Leviathan*,

> is the immoderate greatness of a town, when it is able to furnish out of its own circuit the number and expense of a great army; as also the great number of corporations, which are as it were many lesser commonwealths in the bowels of a greater, like worms in the entrails of a natural man.[32]

As the sovereign must control the militia and town corporations, so also, according to Hobbes as well as Newcastle, must he assert his authority over the sermons, political disputations, and publications of his realm. "It is annexed to the sovereignty," said Hobbes,

> to be judge of what opinions and doctrines are averse and what conducing to peace, and consequently on what occasions, how far, and what men are to be trusted withal in speaking to mul-

---

[31] Thomas Hobbes, *Leviathan* (London, 1651), Part II, chap. 18. C.B. Macpherson, ed., (New York, 1968), 235.

[32] Ibid., Part II, ch. 29, 374-375.

titudes of people, and who shall examine the doctrines of all books before they be published. For the actions of men proceed from their opinions, and in the well-governing of opinions consists the well-governing of men's actions, in order to their peace and concord.[33]

Elsewhere in Hobbes's writing there exists a direct analogue to Newcastle's warning against subjects openly debating the prerogative of the king. Hobbes wrote to Lord Scudamore that "the reason I came away [from England in 1640] was that I saw words that tended to advance the prerogative of kings began to be examined in Parlement."[34]

Hobbes advocated specific laws governing the accoutrements of hierarchy lest the order that ceremony promotes become undercut by inter-class competition.

Considering what value men are naturally apt to set upon themselves, what respect they look for from others, and how little they value other men, from whence continually arise among them emulation, quarrels, factions, and at last war, to the destroying of one another and diminution of their strength against a common enemy—it is necessary that there be laws of honor and a public rate of worth of such men as have deserved or are able to deserve well of the commonwealth, and that there be force in the hands of some or other to put those laws in execution.[35]

Newcastle offered Charles the same advice in the section of his letter entitled "Ceremony and Order." The king ought "to speak to your Heralds," according to the earl,

to set down the ceremony and order for all degrees of your nobility. . .and to have it printed. . .to keep what is only right and due for their places and dignities—as one thing none under the degree of a Baroness can have carpets by her bed and she but one or two at the most [because] now every turkey merchant's wife [has] all her floors [covered] with carpets."[36]

Finally, among many other possible examples of intellectual consanguinity between the two men, Hobbes prefigured the

---

[33] Ibid., Part II, ch. 18, 233. See also Part II, ch. 29, 375.

[34] Thomas Hobbes, Paris, to Lord Scudamore, 12 April 1641. Perez Zagorin, "Thomas Hobbes's Departure from England in 1640: An Unpublished Letter," *The Historical Journal* 21 (March 1978): 160.

[35] Ibid., Part II, ch. 18, 235-236.

[36] Newcastle, "Advice," 211.

economic advice that Newcastle offered his sovereign. On the subject of monopolies, Hobbes wrote, "to grant a company of merchants to be a corporation or body politic is to grant them a double monopoly. . . .Of this double monopoly one part is disadvantageous to the people at home, the other to foreigners."[37] Newcastle likewise warned the king that

> monopolies is [sic] a most horrible thing both to your majesty having but a small sum God knows and here one particular man ingrosses all the trade of that commodity to himself or his own use not suffering any man to trade except he will compound with him and at his own rates and by that means many a tradesman breaks and is undone both [sic] he, his wife, and his children as they did in the monopoly of soap and many others.[38]

One must require, however, more than comparison of parallel texts and mere assertion to establish the connection between Newcastle and Hobbes. Quentin Skinner has rightly observed that Hobbes's philosophy "fitted with a well-marked and by no means particularly sophisticated historical tradition."[39] It would be wrong to assume that his political views were isolated and original theories in his time. There was nothing original about Hobbes's most characteristic political ideas. His only real claims to originality were the reasons he gave for holding his beliefs. Hobbes became the center of philosphical and ideological debate in his lifetime, not because he was the single, unique advocate of a particular point of view. Contemporary opponents attacked Hobbes because his was seen as the ablest and most influential presentation of beliefs that were rapidly gaining adherents and hence ideological importance. Hobbes's *Leviathan* was said to have "corrupted half the gentry of the Nation."[40]

Sir Robert Filmer, among others, shared Hobbes's and Newcastle's penchant for order and their distrust of the multitude. "Many an ignorant subject," wrote Filmer during

---

[37] Hobbes, *Leviathan*, Part II, ch. 22, p. 282.

[38] Newcastle, "Advice," 206.

[39] Quentin Skinner, "History and Ideology in the English Revolution," *The Historical Journal* 8 (1965): 156, 164-165 and passim. See also his "Conquest and Contest: Thomas Hobbes and the Engagement Controversy," in G.E. Aylmer, ed., *The Interregnum: The Quest for Settlement, 1646-1660* (London, 1972), 97-98; and "The Ideological Context of Hobbes's Political Thought," *The Historical Journal* 9 (1966): 295.

[40] Anthony & Wood, "Thomas Hobbes," *Athenae Oxoniensis*, 2 (London, 1691-1692): 278-483. Quoted by Skinner, "Ideological Context," 295.

the 1640s, "hath been fooled into this faith that a man may become a martyr for his country by being a traitor to his prince."[41] Filmer believed that

> there is nothing more uncertain than the People; their opinions are as variable and sudden as tempests; there is neither truth nor judgment in them; they are not led by wisdom to judge of anything, but by violence and rashness; nor put they any difference between things true and false. After the manner of Cattel, they follow the Herd that goes before.[42]

Clearly, then, we need better evidence to establish that Newcastle's advice was uniquely Hobbesian in its content. One might have just as likely found many of the same concepts in the writings of Anthony Ascham, Robert Brady, John Hall, Sir Henry Spelman, or a host of other theorists. One remains especially hard-pressed to establish such links because Newcastle was apparently sincere in his assertion that he read practically nothing during his entire life. His wife lent support to Newcastle's claim in her *Life of the. . .Earl of Newcastle.*

> To school-learning he never showed a great inclination," she wrote, "for though he was sent to the University, and was a student of St. John's College in Cambridge, and had his tutor to instruct him; yet they could not persuade him to read or study much, he taking more delight in sports, then [sic] in learning.[43]

The handwriting, grammar, atrocious spelling, and syntax of the "Advice" all lend credence to the notion that Newcastle, although logical and intelligent, was not a particularly well-educated man. But several sources help to establish beyond doubt the personal Hobbes-Newcastle connection and even a tenuous link between Newcastle and *Leviathan.*

The earliest published letter from Hobbes to Newcastle bears the date 1634. The letter implies Newcastle's patronage of Hobbes well before that time. In January Hobbes wrote to Newcastle that because of inactivity at Court, he would now have "more time for the businesse I have so long owed to your Lordship, whose continual favors make me ashamed of my

---

[41] Sir Robert Filmer, *Patriarcha or the Natural Power of Kings,* edited by Peter Laslett (Oxford: Basil Blackwell, 1949), 55. *Patriarcha* was apparently written in 1642 but not published until 1680.

[42] Ibid., 89-90. Filmer borrows here, of course, the language of the classical writers Thucydides, Xenophon, Livy, Tacitus, Cicero, and Sallust.

[43] Margaret, Duchess of Newcastle, *Life,* 141.

dull proceedinge, savinge that into the number of those favors I put your Lordships patience and forbearance of me."[44]

Most of the correspondence between Hobbes and Newcastle among the Portland Manuscripts bears on the Earl's financial support of the philosopher. Typical of these is Hobbes's letter of August 1635.

> I have received your lordship's guift, proportioned to your own goodness, not to my service. If the world saw my little desert, so plainly as they see your great rewards, they might think me a mountebancke and that all that I do or would do, were in the hope of what I receive. I hope your lordship does not think so. At least let me tell your Lordship once for all, that though I honour you as my Lord, yet my love to you is. . .bred out of private talk, without respect to your purse.[45]

Hobbes also indicated his intention to reside at the Welbeck home of the Earl.[46] Hobbes's letters suggest that he had received an invitation from Newcastle to reside permanently at Welbeck Castle.

The next certain meeting between the two men occurred during the years 1646 to 1648 when Gassendi, Descartes, Newcastle, Hobbes, and the poet Edmund Waller gathered on numerous occasions at the earl's table in Paris. John Aubrey wrote in his *Brief Lives* that "I have heard Mr. Edmund Waller say that the Lord Marquisse of Newcastle was a great patron to Dr. Gassendi, and M. Descartes, as well as Mr. Hobbes, and that he hath dined with them all three at the Marquiss's Table in Paris."[47] Margaret Cavendish, in her *Life* of Newcastle, also mentioned that during his Civil War Parisian exile the earl and "some of his friends, among whom was also that learned

---

[44] Thomas Hobbes, London, to the Earl of Newcastle at Welbeck, January 26, 1633[-4]. Historical Manuscripts Commission, *The Manuscripts of His Grace the Duke of Portland, Preserved at Welbeck Abbey*, 2, 13th report (London, 1893): 124.

[45] Thomas Hobbes, Paris, to the Earl of Newcastle, 25 August 1635. *Manuscripts . . .Preserved at Welbeck*, p. 125. See also Hobbes to Newcastle, 13-23 June 1636 (128); 29 July-8 August 1636 (128-129); 16 October 1636 (129-130); 26 October 1636 (130); 25 December 1636 (130).

[46] Hobbes to Newcastle, 16 October 1636; 26 October 1636; and 25 December 1636. C.H. Firth believed it "doubtful whether the long visit ever took place." Plague, Newcastle's move to London, and the Civil War probably served as impediments to the event, according to Firth, *Life of. . .William Cavendish*, xvi.

[47] John Aubrey, *Brief Lives*, 1, A. Clark, ed., (Oxford, 1898), 349.

Philosopher Hobbes" often discoursed on questions of a scientific and philosophical nature.[48]

In fact, Margaret Cavendish claimed, on at least two occasions her husband corrected erroneous notions of Hobbes,
who used Newcastle's ideas in *Leviathan*. One of these concerned witchcraft.

> They [Hobbes, Newcastle, and perhaps others] falling into a
> discourse concerning witches, Mr. Hobbes said, that though he
> could not rationally believe there were witches, yet he could not
> be fully satisfied to believe that there were none, by reason they
> would themselves confess it, if strictly examined. To which my
> Lord answered, that though for his part he cared not whether
> there were witches or no; yet his opinion was that the confession
> of witches and their suffering for it proceeded from an erro
> neous belief, viz. that they made a contract with the devil to serve
> him for such rewards as were in his power to give them and that
> it was their religion to worship and adore him.[49]

In fact, there does appear in *Leviathan* a passage that accords
in substance with the ideas Margaret Cavendish attributed to
her husband. "As for Witches," Hobbes wrote, "I think not
that their witchcraft is any real power; but yet that they are
justly punished, for the false belief they have, that they can do
such mischief, joined with their purpose to do it if they can."[50]
Whether Hobbes came by this and other ideas in the fashion
recollected by Newcastle and told to his wife remains, however, purely a matter of conjecture. Sir Leslie Stephen, in his
biography of Hobbes, chose to believe that "perhaps the lady
claimed a little too much for her husband."[51] It is not difficult
to imagine, though, Hobbes airing ideas before his friends
while he was working on *Leviathan* and reshaping thoughts in
the light of conversations. The ideas for which Newcastle apparently claimed credit were not of such intellectual stature as
to preclude his conception of them. Neither of the ideas
mentioned by Newcastle's wife contributed substantially to the
central arguments of *Leviathan*. In any event, the important
point stands that Hobbes and Newcastle did over a period of

---

[48] Margaret, Duchess of Newcastle, *Life*, 143.
[49] Ibid., 144.
[50] Hobbes, *Leviathan*, Part I, ch. 2, 92.
[51] Sir Leslie Stephen, *Hobbes* (London, 1928), 36.

years regularly discuss questions of political and moral philosophy during the time that Hobbes was considering the
Leviathan. We can probably safely assume that Newcastle
learned more from Hobbes than vice versa.

The need remains to establish Newcastle's connection with
Charles II; the nature of their relationship that would lead
Newcastle to presume to offer, with some hope of influence,
such a lengthy and detailed piece of advice. Also, in the absence of conclusive evidence that Charles ever read the letter,
we would want to know how it happened that Charles and
Newcastle shared such a temperament that the king would
often act, when he did act at all, in a manner so closely akin to
the earl's advice. How was it, we might ask, that the king and
the earl came to think so much alike? Also, in the light of the
above discussion of the personal and intellectual relationship
between Hobbes and Newcastle, how did Charles come to
share a largely Hobbesian view of the political universe?

William Cavendish was created Earl of Newcastle in 1628
after he entertained Charles I at Welbeck

> in such a wonderful manner, and in such an excess of feasting,
> as had scarce ever before been known in England; and would
> have been thought very prodigious if the same noble person had
> not within a year afterwards made the king and queen a more
> stupendous entertainment, which no man ever after in those
> days imitated.[52]

Such lavishness and the resulting debt (about £20,000) were at
least partly aimed at securing an important Court office.[53] In a
letter to Strafford of 5 August 1633 Newcastle wrote that "I
have hurt my estate with the hope of it. If I obtained what I
desire, it would be a more painful life, and since I am plunged
in debt, it would help very well to undo me."[54]

A letter from Newcastle to his wife dated 8 April 1636
reveals that the specific office he pursued then was the gov-
ernorship of the Prince of Wales. "They say absolutely another
shall be for the Prince and that the king wondered at the report and said he knew no such thing and told the Queen so;

---

[52] Edward Hyde, Earle of Clarendon, *The History of the Rebellion and Civil Wars in England,* W. Dunn Macray, ed., 1 (Oxford, 1888): 167.

[53] E. Mackenzie, *A Descriptive and Historical Account of the Town and County of Newcastle Upon Tyne.* . .(Newcastle, 1827), 46.

[54] *Strafford Correspondence,* 1: 101. Quoted in *Dictionary of National Biography.*

but I must tell you I think most of these are lies, and nobody knows except the King."[55] Another letter told just how stiff the competition became. Newcastle thought that Danby, Leicester, Goring, and the Scots were all serious contenders.[56] Nonetheless, in 1638 Newcastle was appointed the first governor of the eight-year-old prince and made a member of the Privy Council.

Few could have been surprised at the appointment. Newcastle was, according to Clarendon,

> a very fine gentleman, active and full of courage, and most accomplished in those qualities of horsemanship, dancing, and fencing, which accompany a good breeding; in which his delight was. Besides that, he was amorous in poetry and music, to which he indulged the greatest part of his time; and nothing could have tempted him out of those paths of pleasure which he enjoyed in a full and ample fortune, but honour, and ambition to serve the king.[57]

The ultimate significance of Newcastle's appointment was that so many of his personal qualities, beliefs, and interests came to be shared by Charles II.

Newcastle established from the first the habit of writing letters of instruction and guidance to the young prince. As we have seen, the practice continued well into Charles's adult years. One of the early letters bears striking parallels to his "Advice" to the king. Newcastle's "Letter of Instructions to Prince Charles for His Studies, Conduct, and Behavior," written some time after 1638, exhibited in philosophy and attention to detail the same sort of guidance offered in the latter discourse.

Newcastle warned the prince that "whensoever you are too studious, your contemplation will spoil your government, for you cannot be a good contemplative man and a good commonwealth's man; therefore take heed of too much book." The newly appointed governor also instructed Charles to "beware of too much devotion for a king, for one may be a good man but a bad king; and how many will history represent to you that in seeming to gain the kingdom of heaven, have lost

[55] Earle of Newcastle, London, to the Countess of Newcastle, 8 April 1636, in *Manuscripts. . .at Welbeck Abbey*, 2: p. 127.

[56] Newcastle to Countess of Newcastle, 15 April 1636, 1: 127.

[57] Clarendon, *History of the Rebellion*, 8, ch. 83: 381.

their own?"[58] But from what he already knew of the prince, Newcastle believed that Charles seemed already to display a suitable indifference towards books and religion.

What worried the governor most was the formation of good manners by Charles. "The things that I have discoursed to you most," he wrote, "is to be courteous and civil to everybody . . .and, believe it, the putting off of your hat and making a leg pleases more than reward or preservation, so much doth it take all kind of people."[59] A final example exhibits specific concerns expressed in Newcastle's "Advice" to King Charles and passages from Hobbes's *Leviathan* cited above.

> To lose your dignity and set by your state, I do not advise you to do that, but the contrary: for what preserves you kings more than ceremony [?] The cloth of estates, the distance people are with you, great officers, heralds, drums, trumpeters, rich coaches, rich furniture for horses, guards, martialls men making room, disorders to be labored by their staff of office, and cry "now the king comes;". . .even the wisest though he knew it and not accustomed to it, shall shake of his wisdom and shake for fear of it, for this is the mask cast before us, and maskers the Common Wealth. Besides, authority doth what it list. . .you cannot put upon you too much king.[60]

Newcastle resigned his office in 1641 among the tensions surrounding the imminent civil war. Clarendon thought the hostility of Essex and Holland drove the earl to retirement,[61] although perhaps the discovery of Newcastle's complicity in the first army plot was a more provocative cause.[62] He maintained a lively correspondence with Charles during the Civil War years, however, and the prince continued to follow closely the advice and example of his former mentor. Indeed, beginning in 1650, Newcastle served a major role on the Privy Council of the government in exile.

It was during Newcastle's Parisian exile (1645-1648) that he brought Hobbes and Charles together. The earl, still an unofficial supervisor of the prince's education, secured Hobbes's

---

[58] The Earl of Newcastle to the Prince of Wales, [n.d.], Royal Letters in the Harleian Mss. 6988, att. 68. Printed in Henry Ellis, *Original Letters Illustrative of English History*, first ser., 3 (London, 1825): 288.

[59] Ibid., 289.

[60] Ibid., 290.

[61] Clarendon, *History of the Rebellion*, 4: 293.

[62] *Dictionary of National Biography*, cf. "Cavendish, William, Duke of Newcastle."

appointment as a tutor for Charles. It is, however, impossible to know whether Hobbes burdened the prince with much political philosophy at this time.

The prince may have been too young to absorb much philosophy but he could have acquired his appreciation for mathematics and science from Hobbes during their two years together. Charles maintained his interest in the practical application of scientific study and, in fact, may have died as the result of his own experiments with mercury. As king, he granted the Royal Society its charter of incorporation, gave its name, and granted it use of the building and extensive grounds of Chelsea College. Charles also had a hand in the founding of the Mathematical School at Christ's Hospital in 1673 and the building of the Royal Observatory at Greenwich in 1675, both aimed, in the king's mind, at the improvement of navigation. Sorbiere, a Frenchman traveling in England during 1663, expressed astonishment at the scientific knowledge of Charles and the support he gave to scientific enquiry.[63] After perhaps kindling the prince's interests in mathematics and science, Hobbes fell victim to a bout of royal displeasure. Hobbes and the king reconciled their differences, however, and Charles granted and even intermittently paid a pension to the philosopher.

Clearly the impact of Newcastle on the development of Charles's character and personality was much greater than the direct personal influence of Hobbes. In his personality as well as his actions, Charles bore the mark of Newcastle's training. Numerous incidents might be cited as evidence of the shared character traits of the two men. Newcastle's attitude toward his generalship during the Civil War illustrates the point well.

Before he left to join the exiles on the continent, Newcastle raised and commanded an army of about eight thousand men in behalf of Charles I. Of significance here is Newcastle's character in the face of military troubles, a character strikingly similar to that of the later King Charles II. According to Clarendon, Newcastle

> liked the pomp and absolute authority of a general well, and preserved the dignity of it to the full; and for the discharge of the outward state and circumstances of it, in acts of courtesy,

---

[63] Mons. [Samuel de] Sorbiere, *A Voyage to England* (London, 1709), 32-33.

> affability, bounty, and generosity, he abounded; which in the
> infancy of a war became him, and made him for some time very
> acceptable to men of all conditions. But the substantial part, and
> fatigue of a general, he did not in any degree understand,. . .nor
> could submit to, but referred all matters of that nature to the
> discretion of his lieutenant general. . . .In all actions of the field
> he was still present and never absent in any battle. . . .[but] such
> articles of action were no sooner over than he retired to his
> delightful company, music, or his softer pleasures, to all of
> which he was so indulgent, and to his ease, that he would not be
> interrupted upon what occasion soever.[64]

After Prince Rupert's signal defeat at Marston Moor on 1
July 1644, even though he had taken no command in the
battle, Newcastle announced his retirement and intention to
leave England the next day. Clarendon believed that it was
simply because Newcastle "was so utterly tired with a condition
and employment so contrary to his humour, nature, and education," that he resigned so precipitously. Clarendon was
more surprised that he had "sustained the vexation and fa-
tigue so long, than that he broke from it with so little circum-
spection."[65]

Charles exhibited a strikingly similar paradox of character
as a man of action and a lover of ease. It was noted with astonishment by contemporaries that Charles labored like a
navvy, toting buckets of water during the great fire of London.
On the other hand Charles's dallying while the Dutch fleet
sailed up the Thames disgusted contemporaries. "The night
the Dutch burned our ships," Pepys heard that, "the King did
sup with my Lady Castlemayne, at the Duchess of Mon-
mouth's, and they were all mad in hunting a poor moth."[66]

Newcastle's injunctions to the prince against becoming too
bookish or fervent in his religion apparently rooted in fertile
soil. No one, in his lifetime or since, has accused Charles of
having a scholarly nature. Halifax observed that

> his wit was not acquired by reading; that which he had above his
> natural stock by nature, was from company, in which he was
> very capable to observe. He could not so properly be said to have

---

[64] Clarendon, *Rebellion,* 8, ch. 86; 382-383.
[65] Ibid., ch. 80, 380-381.
[66] Samuel Pepys, *Diary,* 21 June 1667.

a wit very much raised, as a plain, gaining, well-bred, recommending kind of wit.[67]

Whether attending the theater, participating in the unending series of Court entertainments, hunting, riding in the races at Newmarket, or conducting Cabinet meetings in his mistress's bedchamber, Charles seemed ever the protegé of Newcastle, never a son of the obnoxiously pious Charles I. Just as Charles's religious indifference contrasted with his father's piety, so too did his womanizing contrast with Charles I's devotion to his queen.

The only tacit criticism the Duchess of Newcastle made of her husband concerned his reputation as "a great lover and admirer of the female sex; which whether it be so great a crime as to condemn him for it I'll leave to the judgment of young gallants and beautiful ladies."[68] Charles notoriously shared the earl's addiction to the company and favors of numerous women. Charles cultivated his social graces, as his governor had encouraged, and never made bitter personal enemies. Most people genuinely liked Charles, although many thought him lazy and too neglectful of public business in the pursuit of personal pleasures. Clarendon, who condemned Newcastle for these same faults as a general, spent much energy scolding the rakish young king whose government he ran.

Evidence that Charles often borrowed books and carried a large trunk filled with them during his travels establishes only the possibility that he read Newcastle's 1659 letter of advice. The closeness of their relationship and the nature of surviving correspondence between them lends credence to such speculation. Charles did read other long letters written by Newcastle, such as the "Letter of Instructions" mentioned earlier. Charles's fondness and respect for his former governor continued unabated into his kingship. Charles's personal instruction by Hobbes suggests a possible knowledge or at least receptivity to the philosopher's ideas. Evidence that Charles shared many social and intellectual traits with Newcastle shows most convincingly, though, the king's pattern of receptivity to

---

[67] Sir George Savile, Marquis of Halifax, *A Character of King Charles II*, in H.C. Foxcroft, ed., *The Life and Letters of Sir George Savile, Bart., First Marquis of Halifax*, 2 (London, 1898); 353.

[68] Margaret Newcastle, *Life*, 149-150.

the earl's advice, the continued closeness of their relationship on the eve of Restoration, and the reason why Charles as king acted in specific compliance with the nobleman's suggestions.

The often close correspondence between Newcastle's advice and Charles's actions as king, adds an extra dimension of significance to the document. Also of importance here are the legislative actions of the first Restoration Parliament during 1661 and 1662. Parliament's attitudes toward correcting the ills of government as illustrated by their actions proved essentially the same as Newcastle's prescriptions in several areas. Not only does the letter illustrate the recrudescence of Cavalier conservatism in Restoration England, but it displays, in the actions of Charles and the Parliament, the active social and political decisions such thought could and did provoke.

With the Militia Acts of 1661 and 1662 and the Act to Preserve the Person of the King (1661) Parliament disavowed any claim to constitutional supremacy. In "An Act for ordering the Forces in the Several Counties of this Kingdom" (1662), Parliament acknowledged that

> the sole and supreme Power, Government, Command and Disposition of the Militia, and of all forces by Sea and Land, and of all Forts and Places of Strength is, and by the laws of England ever was, the undoubted right of his majesty, and his Royal predescessors, Kings and Queens of England.

It further accepted that in the city of London, "these trained bands may again be put to [use] for the safety of his Majesty's person, and for suppressing or preventing of insurrections."[69]

Charles and his ministers were not remiss in this regard, recognizing the fundamental importance of establishing control over the city of London in particular and the military arsenals of the kingdom. The king maintained, just as Newcastle and Hobbes advised, a close and ever vigilant supervision over the London lieutenancy and militia, always careful that they remained in loyal and efficient hands.[70] Also, the Corporation Act (1661) affirmed the king's intention to control the towns and rid them of the "many evil spirits [that] are still working."[71]

---

[69] *The Statutes at Large*, 3 (London, 1770): 219.
[70] J.R. Jones, *Country and Court* (Cambridge, Mass., 1978), 54.
[71] *Statutes at Large*, 3: 213-215.

Charles set out in 1660, as Newcastle advised, to consolidate his position as ruler of England. He moved rapidly to dispose of the large Cromwellian army that remained intact. The army, of course, posed one of the potentially most severe threats to Charles's rule. Parliament's generous general pardon excepting under thirty persons was actively supported by Charles and Clarendon. Such merciful conduct enabled the Crown to disband the army quickly without a serious threat to peace. A small rising in 1661 provided the necessary excuse to retain a much smaller force under the monarch's personal control, also just as Newcastle had called for. Former royalists commanded the militia and received appointments as justices of the peace. Charles and Clarendon elevated the bishops and orthodox clergy to positions of influence in society. They set out with the support of Parliament to secure the total reestablishment of the doctrine and government of the Church of England under its bishops. Only minimal concessions were made to Presbyterians and the sects. The Act of Uniformity (1662) harkened back, just as Newcastle did, to the idyllic reign of Queen Elizabeth, when "there was one uniform order of common service and prayer, and of the administration of sacraments, Rites and ceremonies in the Church of England agreeable to the Word of God, and Usage of the Primitive Church."[72]

To these examples of executive actions and legislative acts of the early years of Charles's reign might be added others illustrative of the shared attitudes of Newcastle with Charles, Clarendon, and Parliament. The two universities were purged and kept under strict control as advised by Newcastle. The earl must have applauded the precipitous fall in numbers of students and the waning of intellectual life in England since he felt there were twice as many students in the universities as warranted and too much attention to books in the nation at large. The Licensing Act (1662) and the Act Against Tumultuous Petitioning (1661) were also in line with Newcastle's strictures against free speech and uncontrolled presses. Another act of 1661 lent strength to the hierarchical structure of society by restoring bishops to the House of Lords and removing the clergy's disqualification from holding lay offices.

---

[72] Ibid., 3: 224-230.

These political actions of 1660-1662 display the receptivity of the first Restoration Parliament to royalist attitudes espoused by Newcastle but effected largely on the initiative of Edward Hyde, Earl of Clarendon and Lord Chancellor from 1660 to 1667. In this they constitute important evidence of the significance of the "Advice" as an expression of the thoughts and rationale that underlay the important political initiatives and widely shared attitudes of the early years of the Restoration. To isolate Charles's attitudes toward government, though, we must look to the later years of his reign. It was especially during the last five years of his life that Charles threw off the shackles of ministerial rule and asserted his own prerogatives as king.

By 1681 the Exclusion question had brought the king and Parliament to loggerheads. It was an event closest in parallel to the confrontation between his father and Parliament during 1640-1641. Charles took his political enemies by surprise, however, and appeared before both houses in full ceremonial regalia. Shaftsbury had no time to organize and *this* king had his Life-Guards and control of the London militia.

Charles was highly displeased at the failure of a London jury to convict the Whig leader on charges of high treason. He therefore remodeled his judicial bench in 1683 to make sure it would never again oppose his will. With the judges behind him, Charles next tackled the municipal corporations, the Whig strongholds, to ensure that the next Parliament would not be filled with his enemies. Many boroughs surrendered their charters rather than risk *Quo Warranto* investigations. Even London sacrificed its charter. A judicial order demanded "that the francise and liberty of London be taken into the King's hands." Charles magnanimously restored all its rights to his capital city on the sole condition that no elected official would in the future take office without his express consent. Charles imposed the same conditions on hundreds of other boroughs that gave him control of the political machinery that elected a majority of the representatives to the House of Commons. In this way Charles solved a constitutional problem that had plagued him since 1660. Indeed, one historian has appropriately termed the closing years of Charles's reign the "Indian summer" of the Stuarts.[73]

---

[73] This account relies heavily upon Roger Lockyer, *Tudor and Stuart Britain, 1471-1714* (London, 1964), 352-354.

In his relations with Parliament, London, municipal corporations throughout England, the lord lieutenancies and militias, the universities, and even the bishops of the Church of England, Charles acted as Newcastle advised. In 1679 the king remodeled his Privy Council along the lines recommended in the "Advice," dissolving the large and unwieldy body and substituting a new type of Council. It was much smaller and included men of varied opinions, even independent and opposition politicians. Charles followed the methods of Elizabeth very successfully among his advisers during the last years. Newcastle would have approved of the way he played on personal rivalries, listening first to one, then another, and always remaining free to pursue his own desires.

It is generally agreed that Charles lived his last years in peace because, as Hobbes and Newcastle predicted, once he silenced his enemies and controlled the military potential of the nation all remained calm. Censorship or fear stifled his opponents after the alleged Rye House Plot. Doctrines of passive obedience to a divinely ordained sovereign echoed from the pulpits unopposed.

It is not my intention in this essay to defend Charles's acts as ultimately just or wise, or even successful, for the history of England. I have hoped only to illustrate the possible origins of values Charles took to his kingship and the widespread acceptance of Newcastle's values among Restoration Englishmen. In this regard I have sought also to establish the significance of Newcastle's long letter to the king. If Charles "neither trusted nor forgave his enemies," as Halifax believed, and seldom forgot personal, if not public service, it was in large measure the result of instructions on conduct instilled in the King from the time he was eight years old and expressed most comprehensively in the 1659 "Advice."[74]

Modern historians have lamented the absence of documents revealing the thoughts of Charles II. Compared to his father and his brother, we know so little about what he believed. Perhaps, in any event, we are safest in judging a man of such duplicity only by his actions. But we do know that a passion for the status quo infected the ruling elites of Restoration England. It was this same passion that filled the pages of Newcastle's letter. Charles, at least, forgot few of the earl's precepts and shared the Cavalier's veneration of the Elizabethan past.

---

[74] Foxcroft, ed., Halifax's "Character of King Charles," 360.

In Newcastle's letter we have the closest surviving statement to a monarchist plan of action on the eve of Restoration.

Newcastle retired from active political life in 1660. The letter was his last political act. He devoted himself to writing plays and poems, encouraging horse racing, and writing his second book on the training of horses. Perhaps the Earl had depicted in his advice a society that became no more than a memory by 1660, but, as David Ogg observed, "in England survivals are long-lived, the sentiment for the past is deeply rooted, and an age is to be judged not alone by the wisdom of the statesman or the originality of the pioneer, but by the less articulate conservatism of the 'ordinary' man."[75]

In the articulate conservatism of the Earl of Newcastle's letter we also see germs of the Tory Party rooted in the old law, religious truth, and political power. Newcastle, in his life and in his "Advice" did not exactly epitomize the strengths of the convervative cause. Neither, of course, did Charles II embody the virtues of Tory conservatism. Both too greatly loved their ease; the former was no general, the latter a poor model for a king. It is Clarendon who rightly deserves renown as his party's single most significant actor among the Cavaliers. Newcastle's letter does, however, personify as no other surviving document the philosophical instincts that underlay the actions of England's ruling conservatives after the Restoration. Newcastle, in his advice, shared with Clarendon a longing to restore England "to its old good manners, its old good humour, and its old good nature."[76]

---

[75] Ogg, *England in the Reign of Charles II*, 1: 147.

[76] Clarendon to Parliament, 1660. Quoted by Keith Feiling, *A History of the Tory Party, 1640-1714* (London, 1924), 69.

Newcastle's Advice to Charles II

The Table

Page

May it Please your Moste Sacred Majestie

I am bold humbley to presente this booke to your Majestie which is writt perticulerly for your Majestie, when you are Inthrond,—why I presente it now is because I thinke your Majestie will have more time & leasure, to reade it now, then when you are Inthrond,—besides it is Intended wholy for your Majesties service, & if it prove so, which I am confident it will, I have my full intention, which service I would not have frusterated by my Death, There is no oratory in it, or any thing stollen out of Bookes, for I seldome or Ever reade any, but these Discourses are out of my long Experience, to presente your Majestie with truths, which greate Monarkes seldome heares, These truths are not only the honesteste, but so the wiseste, that a Dutyfull servante can offer to so Gracious A Master, & so wise a king, as to bee able to Judge———Be-twixte truth, & falsehood, though that———Falsehood bee never so subtley Disguised, I aske Pardon for the method haveing no notes by mee, att All, if your Majestie like it I have my Ends, with———unspeakable Joy, & contentment, if you like it not sr. I humbly begg that favor of your Majestie to ———through it into the fier, that so it may become A flameing sacrefice of my Duty to your Majestie———The Greate God Ever Preserve your Majestie.

For the Militia

I begin with the Militia firste, because it is your Majesties Undouted Prorogative, as also well orderd force, doth Every thing, for without an Army in your owne hands, you are but a king upon a Curtesey of others, and Cannot bee Lasting, where on the contrary you are———Mestroe Dell Campoe, & gives the Lawe & Indeed without Itt, though you are the Su-preame Judg, itt will signefie litle, if you have not power to Determyne, which is Armyes, for otherwise the factious, & faine Disputes of Sophesterall Devines, & Lawyers, & other Philosophicall Booke men, will Raise Rebellions, but not

5

apease them, Therefore I would have your Majestie, have all
your Armes, And Amunition, In your owne hands, & firste to
begin with your Metropolitan Citie of London, that great la-
viathen, that monster, being the head, & that head, so much to
bigg for the body of your Comon wealth of England, so that
Master that citie & you master your whole kingdome, And
your Majestie muste doe itt by two severall ways, firste by
DisArmeing of them, & then By Armeing your selfe, by Dis-
Arming of them totally, in All kindes, no more Citie Captins,
or Collonells, Artilery Yeard, or miletary yeard, & a penalty
upon any that keepes Armes, leaveing them nothing but their
severall watches, in their severall wards, & parishes, to keepe
the streets in order, with their Browne bills, & no more so
much for DisArming of them, Now for your Mejesties,———
Arming your selfe, to over Awe them, & to keepe them In
order, Thus, to have two Royall fortes built on Both sides the
River of Thames, a litle below Greenwitch, Regulated, forts,
like the Citie of Antwerp, or as your Majesties wisdomme Can
beste directe beinge a greate Master In the knoledge of For-
tefications These fortes comandinge the River comandes the
Towne & the Merchantes for feare of their trade will bee In
good order, Then the Tower to bee well fortefeyd, & to bee
your Majesties prime Magasen, for greate store of Armes of
All sortes, both for foote & Horse, with plentye of amunitian,
acomodated by the advise of the beste Soldiers and Ingeneers,
The Tower thus fortefied, will comande both the towne &
thatt parte of the River: Ande thus your Majestie shall tame
thatt Rebellius Citeye, & so consequentlye all Englande thatt
depends off Itt; Itt Is Easeleye dun for their Charter Is for-
feted, and theye will bee glad to take a newe one Uppon your
Majesties Termes——wheras sum disputacius Scoffers will tell
your Majestie this was a thinge this rebellion thatt never hap-
ende before nor never will hapen agen thatt Is more then
theye knowe, howevsoever your Majesties wisdoume Is to
prevent Itt, thatt theye shall nott if they woulde; sum sayes the
kinge Is absolutele to Comande the traynde Bandes (of London), No doubte Legalye butt his Majestie your Father of
blessed memorye was so farr from Comandinge of them as
theye weare the Authors of all his miserye & misfortunes &
faughte moste agaynste him therefore putt Itt nott In their
choyce sr butt In yours & since the Riches & Purse of this

Citeye was the bane and loss of your Royall Father, all fallow-
inge the Purse both by Lande & Seae; Therfore looke to your
Greateste Mischeefe to keepe this Citeye from hurtinge you,
Ande In all thinges butt Armes I shoulde humblye desier your
Majestie to grante them a newe Charter with all their former
priveliges, butt Armes, & to bee kinde & helpfull to them in all
kindes, & to studye the Increasinge of their ritches by the
mentayninge of Trade & never to Violate anye of their Prev-
eliges, Thus your Majestie will bee a gracious kinge, & they
made loyal people, & will Ever bee ready————Hartly to
serve you, & no more to bee preachte, pleaded, or Petitioned
out of their Alleigiance,————for they that have The Armes,
have the purse, & they that have the purse, hath obedience, so
that Armes is all,————

Now for ordering the reste of the kingdome, I would wish
your Majestie to hide your Armes, as much as you can, for
people loves not the Cudgell, though your mastering of London, is some what perspicuous, & Indeed cannot bee helped,
but for the Reste, if your Majestie please to hide your forces in
your porte-Townes, to have them all well fortefied, & good
Garisons In them, both of foote, & horse, such as your Majestie
shall thinke fittest, soe shall you secuer your selfe, from a
forrayne Enemye, & bee able timely to Draw into the feild, a
good Armye againest traytors, & Rebells, should they Rise, &
so bee safe your selfe, & have the bleseing of the people, upon
you, for their peace, & quiettnes, Most of your Majesties porte
townes were Garisons In Queen Elizabeths time, so tis no In-
ovation, an Establishment Made then, for what numbers they
thought fitt, so tis as lawfull for your Majestie now, to add or
Deminish as For Queen Elizabeth, but some sayes the Charg
will bee great, that your Majesites Counsell will very Easely
Setle, As the contentment of the Comon wealth when They
shall playnly perceve their peace, & safely by itt, I am sure
these Rebells, hath puld the skinns over the People eares, for
their perpetual trouble, God forbid your Majestie should doe
the Hundered thousand parte of itt for their peace, but that
Dificultie of Charg will easeley bee setled even by a good, &
wise parlament, That knowes ther can come no mischeefe like
a civill warr, & this will absolutely prevent itt, litle Inconven-
ienceys must bee borne withall & all Doubts Cannot bee solved,

for a foole may doubt more than A wise man Can Answere, some say agen where there Is trade in porte townes a Garison will spoyle itt——How Doth itt spoyle all the trade in Holland, oh but that is in their owne hands say they, why so will your Majesties bee as loth to spoyle trade as they, for tis your Majesties riches, as well as their riches, of the states——Generall, I but sayes some agen they cannot goe In And out where there is a Garison all the Day. I am sure there is no hindering of them, & in the night the Governor sends his keyes presently, & tis Dune, so that these Questions, are but to seeme wiser then their neybours, or that lawyers would not have the Canon law above them,——

Nexte for the Armes of Every County which is cald trained Bands, the question is wethere they should remayne or no. As that they were againest the king your Majesties Royall father, tis true, some of them weare, but itt was where they were forced, with greater power, for many, if not moste, were for the kinge, & served very well in these late times of Disloyall disputations, they questioned wither the king could Remove them out of their county, being only a gard & safety of Every County, but the practice & presedentes shews otherwise, for Queen Elizabeth sent traynd bands In france to Henery the forth, king of France your Majesties Royal Grand father, under the Conducte of the then Earle of Essex, & that was out of their County:——Butt if your Majestie have no traynd bands In every County I know Nott how upon any Insurection how the sheriff with his Posse Comitatus can rayse Armed men, when there is none soe that I conclud that itt is fitt to have traynd bands As they were, & great advantage to your Majestie without Charg so you make well affected Lords, your Lord Leuftenantes, heere I should humbly advice your Majestie never to Joyne Lords in that Commition but Every county to have but one Lord Leutenant, for haveing two Lord Leuftenants joynd, you displease both, because singly they have not the totall Comand And your Majestie had better please one man, then have two men displeased. Besides it will make great faction In Every county, siding with those two Lords, which shall never hartyly agree, & Distracte your Majesties busines, with Cross comands in your Country, & fill your Courte full of faction, in takeing the severall sides which the purse of these Lords will make amongste hungery Courtiers, & brede your

Majestie a great Dell of trouble, & a ground For a pretty Rebellion, Which aught to bee avoyded betimes,———And therefor but one Lord Leuftenant in Every County, & for The traynd bands, thus there is no Danger in them, so long as your Majestie masters London & your porte townes well Garisond, Iff the Londeners should take Exceptions that other Corporatted Townes hath traynd bands & they none, the Case is not a like—Bothe for numbers, or Rebellion, since that Cursed Citie Hath Contrebuted more to this late Horide Rebellion then All England besides, but to satisfie them I thinke itt very Fitt, that no Corporation should have Armes, for they—Are but very few that they are willing to Arme, & as loth they should bee mustered, or Cald out of their towne, So that I conclud no Corporation to bee Armed, but the cheefe Busines is to master London, for so you master all England. And as one sayd what should they bee Armed for, but In times of peace, to play a fooles in finsbury feilds in Trayneing ther. And in time of warr to play the Rebels Againeste their king, so still I conclud master London & you have done your worke, Yett it were better your Majestie had that force in your owne hands, as A troope of horse In Every County proportionable to your County, & some Dragons, which are musketers, & pikes for the Gard of your Amunition, in that County, & but horste upon occasion, & bee sure sr. that you pay the soldere always your selfe by your owne officers, that they may wholy Depend upon your Majestie for other wise it would bee very Dangerous,—The Rebells now know this too well, For they Doe so now which is the wisest way.

The Next is your Majesties Royall Navye & Shipping of England

As God & nature hath made your Majestie the Great Kinge of Ilands & so fitteste for shipping so your Majesties wisedome will multeply your shipping, & mariners All you can, as the old saying is, your Majesties shipping is the Brasson walls of England, a safety at home; & a terror to your Enemies Abroad, a safty at home, wittnes, 88 which a Spanierd remembers to this

Day.————And for a terror Abroad, witnes the rayne of Queen Elizabeth, besides These Rebells that terefies france, makes spayne, makes so Dishonorable a peace, with them, the portugall to Courte them by his Embassadors, & the High & mighty Lords the states of the united provinces, so meanely to Flatter them, that take them selves for the great Lords of the sea & all this foren feare of England Merly for their shipping & nothing Else, there for Your Majestie will studdy that as the principall thing, for your power, & greatnes, & truely were I a Roman & so subiect to non of these following kings, should I be Askte which of the three great kings were the Greatest & most powerful, England, france, or spayne, I would absolutly for truth sake, say the king of England, And merly because of his shipping, which absoluty makes itt. Therefore Increase that which so much Increases your Majesties power over your neyghbors, to write to your Majestie in this poynt is needles. For it would bee a rediculous for men, as for a scoolmaster of a petty scoole, to teach Aristotle, nay more betwixt your Majes-ties knowledg, in Navigation, & myne, which is a great com-forte And Joy to mee, to see your Majestie take Delight in all things that Muste nesesarely make you the greatest & most Glorious Monarch that Ever comanded your three king-domes, a storry tells us That they that have been Ever strongeste by sea, hath Given the Law to their land neyghbors, therefore increase the shipping, firste for your Majesties per-ticuler Royall Navye, increase It Every yeare, both in greater shipps, & Excellent frigatts which will bee moste useful, & your Navye Ever to bee keept In such a condition as they bee Ever Ready, in a very shorte Time, so put to sea, for the Defence of your kingdome, or in ordering of your great neyghbors, for being king of the narrow seaes, that Royalty cannot bee keept by writing of Bookes, as Mare clausu, But by good shipps, to beate their understandings to confess itt, And Queen Eliza-beth was so jealious in that case, as when Henery the forth king of france your Royal Grand father, began to Increase his shipping, shee sent him word, to Disiste for shee would not loose her prorogative of the narrow seaes, & did Assure him if hee did not, Disist, shee would burne his shipps in their Ha-vens, which hee knowing shee was able to Doe, for bore, & lefte that Designe, & itt was most wisely done of her, not to suffer that great king, to Equall her at sea, for then shee knew well that her kingdome might bee in great Danger, The Cardinal De Richlew. His greatest Labor was to make his master great by Sea, And truely hee made so great a progress in itt, by the Neglegence of our state, but your Majesties wisedome will bee Carefull in that Case, not to suffer so great a monarke As a king of france, & so meere a neyghbore, As bee strong by sea, which your Majestie may easeyly helpe at your pleasure, for you are yett thanks bee to God his mastor at sea,——for the shipping of your Majesties kingdom there is nothing will In-crease——Shipping more, then trade, Therefore your Majestie muste keep upp the merchants all that possibly you can, in all places of your kingdome, the Herring fishing would Infinitly increase your mariners, besides the inriching of your kingdome, therefore That business aught to bee moste seri ously, & well considered. The very Cole shipps of Newcastle, in time of nesesety might bee made Excellent men of warr, makeing but porte holes For Cannon, their number being 400 sayle what will all the Merchants shipps of England then bee, their numbers your Majestie may easely have a liste of which is fitt your Majestie should have Every yeare that so your maj-estie might the better proportion them, for your service, ——Sume sayes & to Truely, that the shipping sayleing, nay being against the King your father, was his ruen, truely itt was the Reson the Admirall did not Doe his Duty but put in meane men For Captins, The Remedy these, that follows, to put in Gentle men for Captins, younger brothers, & so they will Bee Imployd, for their Idlenes, & wante, produces Ill conse-quenses In a state, then to have so many lande soldiers, to master The mariners in Every shipp, butt the sureste, & safeste way for your Majestie is to bee master of London, for so your Majestie may bee sure of your Navye, & shipping of your kingdome, for most sertenly they will follow the purpose & your Majestie comanding that There is no feare of the other at all, Thus will your Majestie bee Master both by lande, & sea. Your Majestie muste bee very carefull whome you make Ad-miral, though so long as you master London there is no great Danger. I have harde mr Selden the Lawyer saye that by Land uppon knights fees, your Majestie uppon that Foote Justly might Rayse—60,000 thousand Horse, then Howe many more in your kingdome of England, foote numerously, Then How Great a monarke Is your Majestie both by land & sea

merly by your kingdome of England besides your Majesties
other two kingdomes to boote,—And thus much for the militia by land, & your shipping by sea. I leave it to your Majesties
wisdome & Consideration to thinke what Gards both of foote
& Horse, is fittest to Gard your Majesties Sacred Person, as the
king of france hath, but not so Numerous, besides your Majesties ordinary Gard, & your gard of Pentioners, which I wish
might bee made more usefull To you, the laste, which is the
pentioners, then Ever I saw them, Moste not keeping A Horse,
but Receveing the Pention, which Pention is merely for keeping of horses, And thus much for the Militia In all Kindes.

For the Church

Certeyne Considerations comparing popery, Presbetrye
And the Episcopascy of the church of England In order To
Monarchy.

Monarchy is the Government In cheefe of the whole body
Politick, In all its partes, & Capaseties by one person only So
that if eyther the whole Body Poleticke bee under Any pre-
tennce governed in cheef by more then one severally Itt is no
monarchy.

There bee two mayne partes of Every Body Poleticke Espetially amongeste Christians, *vid:* the state Civill, & The state
Ecleseasticall.

Iff Both thes states, or partes of the Body poleticke Bee not
governd in Cheefe by one, & the same person, They cannot
bee sayd to bee parts of the same Monarcky.

Both thes states are not, nor cannot bee Governd In Cheefe
by one, & the same person, where the state Eclesiasticall Is
Eyther Popish, or Presbyterian, Because the state Eclesiasticall, if itt bee popish, will bee governd in cheefe By non but the
Pope, & if itt bee presbyterian, it will bee Governd by non, but
itt selfe, the one *vid:* Popery Introducing An other Soverayne,
& the other *vid:* Presbytry Erecting an other Soveraynity in the
same body poleticke, & consequently They are both of them
Destructive unto Monarcky.

Neyther can a Prince bee Soverayne so much as in civill
Matters, so long as any other besides himselfe, Eyther abroade,
or att home, Doth claime, & Exersise a soveraynety over the
same subjects, though in pretence it bee but in Eclesiasticis
only.

Because those that pretend to Soverayne Power In Eclesi-
asticalls, muste needs pretende as Indeed both the conclaves
And the Clascis doe pretend to a Soverayne power of Judging,
Like wise, what is Eclesiasticke, & consequently afirming what
They please to bee Eclesiasticall, they may——Governe as
they Please, Even in those things that are meerly Civill.

Soe that Suposing 2: Supreme Distincte Judicatories, the
one Civill, And the other Eclesiasticall in the same kingdome,
as ther muste needs Bee, if Eyther popery, or presbtry, bee
admitted, ther cannot Chuse but bee perpetuall clashing, be-
twixte thes 2: Juresdictions, And the Arbettors of them the
one continually by ther afronting, or undermining or being
afronted, or undermind, by the other, how then shall the
People bee Distracted, to Soverayne powers, at one time in one
kingdome, muste nesesarely so distracte that kingdome, As itt
muste fall into a civill warr.

History will tell your Majestie what sturrs the Pope hath
made In England, & the Presbyterians, much worse, as your
Majestie to well knows, for Indeed, Popery, & presbytery,
though they looke Divers ways, with their heads, yett they are
tied together like samsons foxes by their tayles, cariing the
same fier brands of Covettiousnes, & Ambition, to put all into a
Combustion, where soever they come, that will not submitt to
them.

And therefore as your Majesties Predesesors, to redeeme
them selves From Slavery to the Conclave, did wisely, &
couragiously drive out popery, so itt is not to bee doubted, but
your Majestie that Now is, will to prevent the same, or a worse
bondage to the Classis, with the same wisedome, & courage,
keepe out the Presbetry, As being Indeed a bondage by so
much worse, & more Ignominious Then Popery, by how much
it is worse, to bee subiect to so many tirants,——then to one, &
by how much itt is less Ignominious for a kinge, to bee a vasall
to a forayne Prince, then to the meaneste of his owne subiects.

Neyther is ther Indeed any nesesety, or cause at all, why
Your Majestie or Parlement, should so much as thinke of the

Admittinge Eyther of the one, or other, of those Governments, where wee as I have sayd, the king himselfe, must submitt And become a subiect, when wee are already posest of an Eclesiasticall Goverment, Instituted by the Apostles, receaved And aproved by the primitive christins, Establisht by the Princes, & parlements, of our owne kingdome, pretending To no power over the kinge att all, nor no power under the Kinge, neyther, but from him, & by, him teaching active obedience, to all the Lawfull Comands of Lawfull Authority, And passive obedience, even to those commands that are not Lawfull, so the Authority comanding them bee not unlawful, Forbiding & condeminge all takeing upp of Armes, Eyther offensive or Deffencive, by subiects of any quallyty, or in any Capasety what soever, haveing no Dependencey, or relation to any Forayne Prince, to Protect, or asiste from a broad, nor Any foundation for a People to rise for itt, or with it Att home, but the Church of England wholy & totally Depending uppon your Majestie, Therefore Establish our Establisht religion the Church of England, by so many Princes, & so many Parlements, confirmd both by Gods Lawes, & the lawes of the kingdome, & thus shall your Majestie bee not only an absolute kinge, But pope within your Dominions nexte, & Imediatly after Christe, Supreme head And Governor, & Defender of the true Antient, & Apostolicall Fayth, & you subiects an Easey & sweet Government, In Comparison of the other two, moste Teranicall Goverments Eyther of Popery, or Presbetry.

But methinks I heare some Popishly affected say why not Popery in Englande as well as france, since the kinge of france doth what hee Liste, I Denye that, for they Were forcet to sett upp the Sorbon of Paris to qualafie And order the Pope for the advantage of the kinge, & state, which was a greate trouble to their Goverment, the Popes tireny, And was not Cardnall de Rishlew, laboring itt Extremly, To make a reconsiliation between the Roman Catholikes of France, & the Hugonotts of france, & had gayned many ministers. Absolutely thinkeing to throw of the Hevey yoke of the Pope, And sett upp a Bishopp of their owne to bee Pope of france. This is generally knowne, so to have no dependence of the Pope att all, And though itt coste him much Labor, & mony to gayne the Pope then In being which was Barbaryne, the trouble that hee had with itt Made him Desirious to bee ridd of itt, the Lands are great they

Posses in france, though some princes shares with them, how Many thousand clergye men, & most of their orders, good for Nothing, but Bread Eatters, brings no Honey to the Hive of the Comon wealth, like hornitts, or waspes, brings nothing In time of Peace to the Comon wealth, & will not Defend itt In time of warr.

Sume Sayes Spayne, & the Pope agrees, tis true the Kinge of spayne for the moste parte makes him his Chapline, & so Comonly they Jugle for ther Ends, but I beleeve the king of Spayne was troubled suffitiently, when Pope Barbarine was for france: But howsoever, sertenly if the king of Spayne was head of the Church, within all his Dominions, as your Majestie Is, & the Church Proportiond as your Majesties is, no Doubt but hee would bee a much more powerfull kinge then hee is. For Presbetry itt is as Distructive, to Monarcky as uncomly in itt, & a litle to fancy with God Allmighty sans seremony, but lett any tell mee where any monarcky Is, where itt is, planted, nay where they are but alowed As in france, what worke have they made, how many civill warrs, untill Cardnall Richlew, tooke order with them In takeing a way all their strong holdes what Civill warrs Have they made in Germeney such Combustions. Therefore I conclud sr. absolutly the church of England both for the Quiett of your Majestie & your subiects. Some will say In poynt of Gayne to In Rich your Majestie to take Bishopricks, & Church Liveings away, that sertenly is misunderstood, for their Lands being all in Lease will not bee sold for much, & what with firste Frutes, Duble Subsidies, & many other things, your Majestie will not loose much in poynte of Profitt, for when one BB: Dies you may Remove moste, & in Goverment & being. Absolute kinge you will loose very much, for it was sayd moste truely no Bishopps, no King, for our late troubles Hath Justyfied that saying to much, that the subvertion of the Bishopps would bee an advantage to the Comon wealth, Is very false, for now all the BBs:, Denes, & Chapters, Estates, Are in the hands of the Layetey, the tenents at moste Easey Rates, & almoste as good as Inheretence, & should they fall Into Laye Lords hands, their tenants would Curse the time That made them soe.

For the Bishops sitting in the upper house, sertenly, they Have as much, & as Antiente right of sitting there, as any Peere of the Ralme, for though it is the Inheretence of a peere of the

Relme, & to his posterety, yett that Lords posterety may Fayle, but a Bishopps seae never, Exsept roote, & branch, Bee puld upp, as in these rebellious, & wicked times, And since All the Bishopps depend uppon you, tis no Disadvantage to your Majestie to have them sitt in the house, tis not the three Estates if the Bishopps bee out, for it is the Lords spirituall, Temporall And Comons.

Now for the Bishopps they should bee Chosen wise men for Goverment, rather then Scoole Devines, & not to make A Numerous Clergye, for a litle mony to their Secretaried, to undoe our Church, & Comon wealth, for where There are not Liveings for those ministers they muste of Nesesety run into Lecturers, for their Lively hood, & as Nesesarely to please their benefactors, preach Sedition, In Church, & Comon wealth, & preach downe the person of the parish, & make him bee Despised, & then they thinke They have Done their worke, therefore to proportion the Clergye according to the Liveings that is for them, with a smale over plus; & to alow of no Lecturers, which muste bee the Bishopps care, & to make no minister that is not orthodoxe to the Church of England, for your Majestie knowes by too woefull Experience that these Lecterors, have preachte your Majestie out of your kingdomes, & with Ill preaching to, but with great sedition, And faction, & Indeed the Lectorers one of the greatest Causes of our Late miseries, therefore no Lectorers, att all, in no place Then I should wish that these Bishopps In their severall Diaseases might moste carefully looke into Scoolemasters, from the petty Scooles, to the Gramer Scooles, that they bee orthodoxe according to the Church of England, & so to Educate their Puples, for sertenly as wee are bred of that Religion or opinion wee are of, for the moste parte, if your Majestie please To Looke with unpartiall Eyes uppon the whole world you shall finde itt soe, therefore this poynt aught to bee very Carefully Lookt into, & not weavers to teach petty Scooles, And Expound the Bible, which hath added much to our miseries, And Even the females, all Girles muste goe to the same petty scooles for if they bee Infected with a weavers Docterine, att firste, they will infecte their Husbands afterwards, Therefore no teaching of scooles, Eyther petty or Gramer scooles, but such as the Bishops shall alow of & thinke Fitt.

The Nexte is great care of the universities, no heads of houses, But orthodox, nor no studente that is of an other

opinion Butt Expell him the universety, for such milke, as they
sucke Firste, their norishment will be accordingly, & if itt run
cleere att the Spring head, it will bee cleere all the way And
thus your Majestie in a little time, will bring your Church In-
sencibly as you would have Itt, for as wee are bred, so wee live,
& so we Dye, for the moste parte. No minister to have above
one liveing, to preach Every Sunday, & Holly Day, & but once,
& to Catechise in the After noone But I should wish no man to
preach his owne sermons, but such as our Reverend Bishops
should approve of, that is, as so many Homilles for the proper
Sundays And Hollydays, for the Compas of a yeare, to bee
made, & printed, And so sent to Every person of the parish to
bee preacht And to prach no other, & those Sermons to preach
Jesus Christe, our Salvation, Godly Life, to avoyd sinn, & Ex-
ercise Charety, & perpetually to Instruckt the people, of their
obediences to their superiors, & Governors, withall the respecte that may bee, Nay the Catechising to bee printed, as well
as the Sermons, for otherwise they will take Liberty ther, Thus
shall your Majestie bring great quiet to your selfe, & your
people, In not Disputing your right, & prerogative in pulpetts,
to Inflame the people with Disobedience, or rayle of their
Governors, & Every Sunday to make Libels of them in their
Sermons, & when once Authoryty is Dispised, what can follow
But A Civill warr, the Emperor of Russia findeing the People
apte to Comotions, being sturd upp by the pulpetts, made a
Lawe, that non should preach any sermons, but what was
Deliverd by the Bishopps, to the ministers, & printed, &
Braught a great quiett, & Setlement to his kingdome only by
this meanes, I doe not meane that Bishops, or Denes, should
bee tyed upp, or a perticuler favor from the Bishops sume-
times, to some that are Discrett, to Preach sometimes, butt
otherwise all to preach nothing But the printed Sermons,
wherein your Majestie & your People, will finde great Ease &
quiett. Itt is very fitt for the Bishop of Canterbury, & the
Bishopp of London, to bee of your Majesties privey Counsell,
to sitt there still for what may conserne the Church, or the
Scooles, but no more Bishopps of the Counsell, not no Bishops
to bee made Lord keeper, Lord Treasurer, or any other Laye
office, nor no Devine a Justice of Peace, for itt is very Im-
proper, they should medle with Any thing, out of the Church,
But the great Inconvenience is that when Bishopps are made
great officers, & Devines Justices of Peace, itt Rayles so much

mallice, & Envie In the Noblety, Gentery, Lawyers, & Comons, as they never reste untill they pull them Downe, & ruine the Church, as your Majestie hath seen by our Late, & woefull Experience, when of the other side, the Clergye not medleing in Laye Busines, the Lords, Gentery, & Comons are so farr, from being against them, as they are for them, & the Church not being proude, And Haughty, over the Layety, but Gentle, & Curtious to them, the Layety will upphold the Church, not intrenching one of An other, but Each of them, kept In their severall Circles, will peacebly Joyne to Serve your Majestie in a happy Harmony for your Government, where ther are many vicariges, itt were fitt they should bee made upp at 200^c A yeare a peece for worthy men to inJoy them, but from whence this mony should Come, is the poynte, to force the Layety to sell their Impropreations, were as great an inJustice as to sell any of the reste of his Inheretance, for soe is his Impropreation, The Layety made them not so neyther, but the Pope, at the petition, of the Abotts, to have them nexte to their monesteries, & when The Disolution of the Abyes fell, their Apurtenances, which were The Impropreations, fell with them. Henery the 8th did not Begin this, butt Cardinall wolsey gott an order, or decree from The Pope, to Demolish so many Abyes, for the building of Chrise church in oxford, & Else where, & itt may bee itt Helpt to build white Hall, which was the Cardinalls House belonging to the Seae of yorke, itt may bee those——Monesteries helpt to build Hamton Courte to, which was Cardinall wolseys house also, soe your Majestie sees Henery the 8th followed butt the Cardinall & the Pope, as his presedents, & I wish that Henery the 8th had never dune a worse thing, then pulling Downe the Abyes, for those Abyes, Coverd with seeming pietty Much sin, & weckednes, besides Devoering so much of the Comon Wealth; Litle Serveing itt at any time, But Enough of this, if not to much, for itt yett stickes in the stomachs of moste of our Clergy,—But to Increase the vicarages to a 100th a yeare Att Leaste, for worthy men, to live of them, is the busines. A Bishopp told mee, hee thought itt might well bee made out of the Bishopricks, there is an other way may bee added to itt, which is a house in Phillipe Lane, Called Sion, founded by Doctor White, which did more hurte in the Church, then Any thing I know, for there they mett, sertene Days in the weeke, so many ministers had a full good

Diner, & there They would apoynte whoe Should preach att
moste Churches In London, the revenuse that came into bye
out Impropreations of great value, & this being in the Presbeterians hands, the Apoynting the ministers to preach, sowed
Sedition, & the mony And Impropreations they baught, In,
mentayned sedition, so that if your Majestie take itt into your
owne hands, & apoynt Honest, & wise orthodox Devines,
Comitioners, to order that Busines, for the benefitt of the
Church, & the Bishope of London supervisor, it will bee advantagious to Gods Church, & your Majesties Govermente,
starveing the presbeterians, & better feeding of Christs
Church, In augmentation of the vicarages. Here I humbly
offer to your majestie that hee that you make Bishopp of
London, might bee both a wise, sturring, & stoute man, And to
Preach often, amongste them, sturring, because The Citie is
great, & subiecte to many sectes, & Sisemes stoute to punish, &
wise in Doeing itt Discretly, And For preaching it will take that
Citie very much, Being given so much to preaching, sertenly
the Colidg caled Sion could not have apoynted preachers in
London had the Bishopp of London Carefully, as hee aught to
have lookt unto Itt. Thus the parson of Every Parish to preach
Every Sunday, on printed Sermons, in the fore noone & to
Cathekise out of the printed Cathekisme, in the afternoone,
And Every Holly day, to preach such printed sermons, proper
for those Hollydays, & no Lecterors, or other times for service,
on the weeke Dayes, will bring your majestie, & your people, A
great Dell of quiett, the Roman Catholikes, makes so many
Holly days by their numerous Saynts, as poore treadsmen And
Laboring men, cannot Live off their Severall Callings for
them, & the Presbyterians, so many severall Days in the weeke,
with their Exersising, & Prophosing as itt undoes poore people, takeing them from their callings, as much as the Roman
Catholikes doth, but the Church of England is so well ordered,
in neyther to few, or to many Hollydays, Eyther one way, or
other, as it is sufitient For the publike service of God, & not to
Distracte the Comon People, from their Livelyhood. For God
apoynted six days to Labor, & the seventh to reste, & serve
him, so In obedience to that, & many Hollydays to boote, wee
have, which is suffitiente, The Bible In English under Every
weavers, & Chamber maids Armes hath Done us much hurte,
that which made it one way is the universitys Abounds with to

many Scollers. Therefore if Every Colledge had But halfe the Number, they would bee better fedd, & as well Taught, Butt that which hath one moste hurte, is the Aboundance of Gramer Scooles, & Ins of Courtes, the Tresurer Burleygh sayd ther was to many Gramer Scooles, because itt Made the Plow, & the Carte, bee neglected, which was to feed us, & Defend us, for ther are few that can read, that will putt Their hands to the Plow, or the Carte, & Armyes are made of the Comon solders, & ther are very few that can read, that will carry a muskett, & ther are so many scooles now, as moste read, so Indeed there should bee but such a proportion, as to serve the Church, & moderatly the Law, & the merchants, & the reste for the Labor, for Else they run out to Idle, & Unnesesary People that becomes a factious burthen to the Comon wealth, for when Moste was Unletterd, it was much a better world, both for Peace & warr. Every Sunday, & Hollyday, after Devine Service, Lett the People a Gods name, have their Lawfull Recreations. For seremoney In the Church it is a nesesary as any thing, for though Seremoney, is nothing in itt selfe, it doth Every thing. Itt keepes upp Gods house, the kinges, & the Comon wealth, for with out itt, ther is no distinction & then ther muste bee confution, without seremoney what is our Church, of England comed to Nothing, what is our late king comed to, martherd, without seremoney what is our Lords comed to, Dispised, & nothing, without seremoney, & Gentery Loste, & Every thing in confution. Therefore Juste such seremoney as the Church of England teaches which is not so much as the Roman Church, which uses so many pupett Playes, as makes itt rediculoius to the People, nor so litle as the Presbyterians, as almoste takes away the peoples Reverence in your Majesties church, & all Cathedrall Churches, according to the Church of England, & in all Cathedrall Churches, according to the Church of England, & in all other Churches, according to the Lawes of the Relme, & not to force any thing beyond itt, as the Comunion Table to stand alter wayes, or otherwise, according to the Lawes of the Relme, How many Bookes was written aboute the standing of the Comunion table, which was one thing, that began our troubles, as one sayd merely, ther was much adoe aboute the standing of the table wither it should stand like A Dreser table, or a shovellbord table, itt is not how the Table stands, but how the Communicante worthyly receves that Holly Sacrement of the Lords Supper, with all reverence, & seremoney, so that your Majestie muste see that all Desente Seremoney bee deept upp in the Church, or Else the Church will fall to nothing, as itt hath Latly Dune. Then no Disputations butt in Scooles, nor no bookes of controversey, writt butt in Latin, for Else the People would bee over heated with itt, for controversey is a Civill warr with the Pen, which Pulls out the sorde soone afterwards.—all prayer Bookes & Bookes of Piety, In English, & non Else, & all Bookes whatsoever Is written Eyther by Devines, or Philosophers, or any that may Make the Leaste rente In Church, or state, presently to bee Condemnd, & burnte by the hands of the Hangman, & the Authtors severly punisht, Even to Death, if the Crime requier itt. For your Majestie aught to bee very watchfull, & carefull in This poynte, for here Justice is great Clemencey, & mercy For a few to suffer, rather then so many Distroyd in a civill warr,—& your Majestie muste looke bee times to itt, as soone as Itt peepes towards a sedition, for in the beginnings, itt is easey to Supress that which when itt hath taken a head, itt may supress your Majestie. The Bishopps should looke that all noble mens chaplines should bee ortho-dox. And in all Eclesiasticall Courts, they should bee Gentle, to the Layety, & not to Excommunecat For Every tith Sheafe, or bee Litigius, for that will never Gayne the People, but the Contrary, & in Excomunication is a thing of a High nature, & therefore to bee used but in Exterodinary Cases, & for goeing to Lawe, for Every tith Egg the parson will Loose by itt in the End, for when itt is tryed, by a Jury, itt will Pinch of the parsons side, A parson told mee, that being kinde to his Parishoners, they would bring home all his tiths both Haye & Corne, his fewell both woode, & cole & Indeed doe Any thing for him hee Desired, for if hee bee a wrangling Parson, the Publike purse, will bee to hard for his privatt Purse, & the Jury of Country men, will bee for the parish, Lett him preach what hee will, so for this world kindnes Is the beste, for the parson, & Charety, & Love, for the nexte, Sertenly,—Some will say that the Pride of our Church Did over throw itt, I Doubt ther was to much of itt. And some wondering at itt, some sayd the Pride of their Learning made them unJustly thinke all others fooles, when the old saying is, the greatest Clarkes are not the wiseste men, sum agayne sayes, that haveing been Scoole masters, And

Tutors, in universities, to their Puples, & the Imperiall
Comand they have had over Boys makes them thinke all The
Layety Are to bee used like boys, but the Layety hath wipte
them out of the Church, some againe says if they Reade storry,
& Cesaers Comentarys, that they are greater soldeiers then
Cesar, Pompey, Brutius, Caseus, did no good at All againest
Cromwell, & Ierton, for any aplycation I Ever Hard they could
make,—Itt is not bookes, butt practice That Doth all in this
world, Butt howsoever I should with them, that which they
preach moste, which is Humilety & To forgive, which some
sayes Scollers are unapte to, some thinks because they are not
suffered, such privatt revenges As the layety hath,—But sertenly I thinke these were Scandalls Layd uppon our Church, to
pull itt Downe, then that itt was Truth,—& when God, & your
Majestie restores our Church, I make No Doubte but your
Clergey by their wise Demeaner, & Carige will prove all these,
Moste false, & scandelous aspertions, By their Humilety and
other personall virtues, & Every bishopp in his severall Diases,
should bee your Majesties faythfull Intelegencers, what Bap-
istes, are in their Diases, what Presbytarins, & other sismatickes, what Scoole masters, & How the Noblety, & Gentry, are
affected, & what riches, & what power they have, which the
People, & Even the Dispotions of the people. So the Chancelor
of Each universety, by his vice Chancelor, nay to have other
privatt Doctors, spies over Their Goverment, whoe are heades
of houses, to Informe where any thing is a mis, & the Chan-
celors to informe your Majestie so the severall Bishopps to
Informe his Grace of Canterbury, or London, & they to Informe your Majestie that which hath Dun much Hurte in our
Church is This, in Queen Elizabeths time old Burley favord
the Puretan, faction to much, so did Secretary Walsingam,
And the Earle of Lester, that great favoritt, then had a Plott to
pull downe the Bishopps had not good Whitgifte the Bishopp
of Canterbury stood in the Gapp & saved our Church, & God
knowes his power was not so great As all good men wisht him,
after this the Earle of Essex, that was beheaded, followed the
tracke of his father in Lawe, Leaster, In favoring the Puretan
party, afterwards as They sayd the Late Duke of Buckingam
favord the Puretan Faction, & had the greatest puretan to ride
in the Coach with him, & my Lady his mother, a Roman
Catholike to keepe upp that party, & my Lady his sister to

keepe upp The puretan party, & that the poore Church of England was squesed between these two factions, held upp by the Powerfull favoritts of Courte, for their state Ends which hath brought us to this woefull misery, that moste Excellent person mr Hooker had not writt his Eclesiasticall Polesey, but that the Puretans troubled the state then in Queen Elizabeths time, & therefore shoud have been Lookt to in time, & not have been held upp by the great ones, Your Majestie must have an Exacte account what Semenarry prists, Jesuitts, & friers, are in England, Scottland, & Ireland, which your Majestie may Easeyly have, not only by the Information of the Purseuants, Butt by Some false Brothers, a mongste them, besides there will many fall to our side, Eyther for Contience, or Gayne. which will well Inform the Bishopp of Canterbury, & hee your Majestie in that Busines,—They say Secretary Walsingam-mayntaynd young Scollers in most of their houses beyond Sea to give him Intelegence of all the English prests, their names, Dispotitions, Digneties, & Designes, as farr as they could Learne,—And so if the Roman Church In generall, nay I have hard that sr francis walsingam had two Cardinalls feede his att Rome which was much, when ther was such an open Detestation of the Pope, in England, then,—the puretans & sismeticks there are Laws suffient to punish them, if they bee putt in Exsecution,—as in the beginning of our Bible your Majestie may see By actes of Parlement, I thinke in Edward the 6th time,—Renewed in Queen Elizabeths time, & so in king James your Majesties Grandfather of Blesed memory, yett I know your Majesty will have a great care of tender Contiences, Butt sr. there is nothing can so well Setle the Church And keepe itt In order as the Power to bee in your owne Hands, which Is the Drum, & the Trumpett, For Disputts will never have an Ende, & make new And Great Disorders, butt force quietts all things, And so this A mongste the Reste.

For the Lawe

In time of Popery, the Church Did swell so much as itt Became Hedropicall, & would have Distroyd the whole kingdome, & Devored itt, had itt nott been Lookte to In time, witnes the Lawe of Morte-men, for had not that been, Dieing men, what would they not give to purchase Heaven, att that pinch, & had not that Lawe, then have been made, & putt in Exsecution, that very thing, would have att length purchased all the kingdome, Into the hands of the Eclesiasticks.

After the reformation, & Disolution of the Abyes, then the Lawe crepte upp, & att laste grewe to bee so numerous, And to such a vaste Body, as itt swelde to bee to bigg, for the kingdome, & hath been no smale meanes to fomente & Continue this late & unfortunate Rebellion. Howe to Deminish them would bee a hard worke, they have taken So Deepe roote in England, to Lessen their fees will not Doe itt, fewer Gramer Scooles would Doe well, for if you Cutt of much reading, & writing, their muste bee fewer Lawyers, & so Consequently Clarks, which I have been credibly Informde, that ther are: 60,000: clarkes at leaste, what Number of Lawyers then, the Nurseries of them should Bee Lookt unto, not to bee to many, what abundance of Ins are ther, as Furnevalls In, staples In & God knowes How many. There should bee suffitient, but not an overplus, And that would a bate them, howe was itt heeretofore That in the Courte of Comon Please, where ther are none Butt Serientts admitted to pleade, that in those Dayes There was butt one Seriente, & hee pleaded, both for the Playntive, & Defendante. As now if itt please your Lo:ps for The playntive, & when hee had done that, then after hee began, may it please your Lo:ps now for the Defendent, & now ther are so many serientes, so many of the Coyfe, as they are not able to stand at the Comon Pleaes Barr, & their fees being so Great, Drayns the purses of the poor subiecte, being forcet To have so many of Counsell of Each side, & att Every call of Serients, Every seriente pays your Majestie £500 a peece, which your Majestie never hath, but some Courtiers, so your Majestie had Better give a £1000: a peece, then make them, both for your owne sake, & your poore subiects, for your owne sake, when they are Advanced to bee serients, they presently thinke of higher And greater pleaces, & being so many serientts, they cannot All bee prefered, neyther are they all worthy, those that Are not preferd, then they muteney, & strive to Doe your Majestie All the mischeefe they can, under the pretence of Lawe, & will Bring your very prerogative in Dispute, out of reveng, & hope of preferment, which was once their way. Thus itt Doth Hurte your Majestie & for hurting your poore subiects itt Drayns their purses, some of them to begery, I have hard many say, that the Chancery heretofore, had but very few Causes Judged ther, And now of Late I have hard, the subiecte much complayne of itt, as one of the greateste grevances of the kingdome, for sayes The subiectes there is Lawe, & chancery, if one side have the Better, in the Lawe, the other party bringes him presently into the Chancery, for the Chancery aught to Doe nothinge againest the Lawe, Butt to mitegate the Rigor of the Lawe, but uppon this truth, There is never a cause, in any Courte of England, but firste, or Laste, itt Comes into the Chancery, & then God knowes howe many yeares it may bee ther, as many sutes have been, This the subiecte complayns of much, & I wish itt were Redreste, & that no sute what soever should continue Above a twelve month att the Longeste, Eyther in the Chancery, or any courte Else, This would Ease the poore subiecte mightly. But your beste Counsellors & advisers In these Cases is a wise & Holsome parlemente, that would setle all things to your Majesties contentment & the contentment of your Loyall subiectes, Some says there Are so many Lawyers in the house, as would obstruct any Thinge that is againeste their profitt, truely I doe not Beleeve that, for sertenly there are many wise, worthy And Honorable persons that belongs to the Lawe, that would Rather bee for the Publike good, then a private, & perticuler Benefitte. Some Sayes agen, that ther is no man fitt to Bee Lord keeper, or Lord Chancellor, which have been two Distincte offices, heeretofore, Butt a Comon Lawyere, their Reson is this, say they if the Lord Keeper is to Doe nothing Againeste the Lawe, butt only to mitigate the Rigor of itt, if Hee bee not a Lawyere, how shall hee knowe what to doe, when hee Doth not know the Lawe, they say well, But yett itt may bee Answered, that one that is no Lawyere May bee a very good Lord keeper, as there hath been In Former times, both of the Church, & Gentery, haveing Always Judges to assiste him, for poynte of lawe, as hee, May call out of any Courte, what Judges hee pleases, Nay some great Lawyeres have don so often uppon some Greate Causes, knowing the Lawes as well as the Judges that Hee sent for, some scandelous people, would say, hee only sent for the Judges, only to hide his corruption, but I hope Itt was for a better Ende. But truely In my opinion I doe thinke a Lawyere absolutly is the fittest man to bee Lord keeper.

Then the Courte of Requests, when the Earle of Manchester was privy Seale, hee made so considerable, as being so full off Causes, as the Lord keeper Complaynd of itt, for the kinges Bench, that Courte properly belongs to the Crowne, both Criminell, & Civill, for the Exchecker, that properly belongs To your Majesties Revenues, & I have hard many say, that there Are such abundance of officers belonging to that Courte As itt is much to your Majesties preiudice, as well as to the commonwealth Butt I have hard the Lord Coventry that was Lord keeper of England, whoe was both a wise man, & a good Lawyere, & well Practiced in the Checker, affirme, that though many went A boute to Alter the Goverment, & Custume of that Courte That all the witts in the world, could not posibley order itt better, Then itt was but was forcet always att Length to fall backe To the old Goverment for your revenues itt were very requisitt that your Majestie Had an understanding Honeste man, to your Tresuror, if there Bee such a one to bee founde, that will studdy your Majesties Profitte, more then his owne, I hope your Majestie may finde such A one, butt never any kinge, or Queen, did, that Ever, I hard of that profittable place, is a greate temptation To Honesty, And as the Earle of Strafford told mee, that iff the Lord Tresuror would stretch his Contience, that hee Mighte gett the Divell & all, & I never hard of any Lord Treasurors Contience, but was of streatching Leather. Your Lord Treasuror may tell your Majestie that the times being so Nesesitous, that the Place is worth Litle, or nothing, in which Hee Doth falsefy with your Majestie for the more nesesetus the times Are the greater profitt to the Tresuror, as for Exsample, putt The Case there is £40,ooo: oweing, & hee hath butt £20,000: to pay, And those that are to bee payd, knowing this full well For hee will tell them so, whoe is such a foole then, that will not give halfe, to have Halfe, rather then to have Nothing, & hee that gives moste, the Tresuror heretofore Payd, & the whole Debt, acknowledg, by that man to bee payd This is but one way, of thousands, that the tresuror hath to Inrich himselfe, as to make new bargins in the Custome house to advance your Majesties revenues, some smale inconsederable thing, And fill his owne purse, as also out of your Majesties Lands, and words, & all forfitturs, the truth is if

the tresuror, bee Nott an Intier Honeste man, they play with
your Majestie as in Ben Johnsons Alcamiste, the Tresuror is
Doctor Subtle And his Chancelor Captin Face, Then hee hath
Newyeares Gifts to boote, which is no smale thinge, I have
hard when The Earle of Dorsett Died that was Tresuror, that
gott Extreamly, & then the Earle of Salsbury was made Tresuror, And when king James had made him, after his Humble
thanks for the favor, hee told the king that hee would not sitt
all Newyeares Day, to receave Newyeares giftts, Hee would
promis him that, & hee kept his promis, For hee always
apoynted, 3 or 4 Days after to receave them. The Lord St.
Albones, being told that his place was a vaste place of Gayne,
hee told them very modestly that truely his Newyeares giftes
were good, hee would Nott call them Bribes, the Lord keeper
is a vaste place Indeed, for all the kingdome comes with his
hands to bee used As hee pleases. For when Hatton was
Chancelor, being No greate Lawyere, hee had one Doctor
Ducke, that stood Always by him, to helpe him, & the Counsell
pleaded so Excellently on both sides, as very much troubled
the Chancelor, how to make a Decree, so the Chancelor, told
Doctor Ducke, itt was a very Dificult busines to judge, the
Doctor Answered very Easey my Lord, says my Lord how is itt
Easey, marry sayes the Doctor, because it is as pleases your
Lordship & itt is true, Every thing is as itt pleases his Lordships, & then I doe not know how his Lordships should be
displeased, duering the holding of that place, Pardons will bee
a vaste sum to him, & so to the Aturney, Now For the Duckeye
that Courte was Erected for Lankester In John of Gants time I
take itt, & though those lands Are returned to the Crowne yett
the Courte still holds For the Courte of wards, that Courte is a
greate revenue, To your Majestie if itt bee well Handled, so I
shall only humbly Advice, not to Lessen your Majesties revenues att all, but to Have such Comiseration of your poore
subiects, that wards May not bee baughte, & sold like Horses in
Smithfield, All their woodes cutt downe, their Estates Ruined,
& your Majestie not the better, therefore if there might bee
such A Course taken, that your Majestie may have the Benefitt,
& the ward not Ruined, for many houses have been uterly
Loste, & no one by war shipps, This care would become your
Majesties Gracious favor to your subiectes, where they would
Always pray for, & Blese your Majestie for itt, what vaste

Estates hath Lord keepers Lord Tresurrors, & masters of the wards, Gott, old Burgley raysed two Earles, & a viscounte, of great And vaste Estates, besides many more of his famelly, both Male & female, Now for the star chamber, ther was Great exceptions to that, as an Arbetrary Courte. Tis true itt hath not been very Antient, but sertenly The Intention, & foundation, of itt, there Could not Posibly bee a better, for before that Courte was Erected, what disorders, what Riotts, was Comitted Dayly, Even to Disorder the Judges of Asises where they satt with munmoth Capps, Baskett Hilte sords, & Blewe Cotes, take the partes of their masters, when their masters, had any Difference one with an other, And after the star chamber was Erected So much peace, & quiettnes, to your Majesties people, as any man Might have ridd with a riding Rodd all through your kingdome, without any trouble, or molestation to him, so litle use There was of a Lord, & all that quiett, & tranquilety, by That Excellent Courte of star Chamber, Tis true, there May, bee an abuse of any thing, & so of that Courte, but because There was an Abuse, therefore should that Courte bee taken away God forbid, the abuses should bee rectefied & The Courte remayne by that Rule because there is often And to often an Abuse of Holly writt, should the Bible Bee taken a way, no sertenly, butt the abuses mended, And Every thing should not bee brought into the star chamber, Butt only those Causes that are proper for itt, neyther should they strive to make your Majestie a Revenue out of the sins of the people, that was not the Intention of Erecting That Courte, the peace of the kingdome is your Majesties Cheefe Ende, & for the fines God knowes they add litle to your Majesties Revenues, but Comonly some Courtier or other begges them And your Majestie hath Litle or nothing, but they that find falte with this Courte, & all Arbitrary Courtes, is because the Lawyers would have all things reduced to the Comon Lawe, so that they might have more Corne Come to their Mill & those that Speakes most againest itt, what Doe they when those Courtes are down, but to Erecte severall Comittes, to stand Instead of itt, which is ten times worse, the same thing, but worse with a new name. Therefore this Courte of Star chamber is Excellent, They will say Indeed whoe soever Comes there if hee scapes a broken peate, hee is sure to have a Scratcht Face, but one should Aske him why hee comes there, Then there is your Majesties pres-edents both of wales, & of the North, which are both most

Excellent Courtes, being Much for your Majesties Honor &
Safety, for quietting of your People, & a great Ease unto your
people, Lett them say what they will, for poore men are able to
goe to ludloe, or yorke, when they are not able to goe to
London, As the Phrase is, I will make you water your horse att
High Gate, by my fayth that goes hard with poore Men, Some
sayes Lawyeres, are againest both these Courtes, to oute the
same former resons, I told your Majestie I had forgot two
thinges that your Majestie will bee pleased to have a care of, &
itt is in the Lord keepers office, The firste is what Church
Liveinges soever there is under £20 In the Kinges bookes, all
those I say, are in the Lord keepers Giftes, The Nexte is hee
hath the makeing of all the Justices of peace In England, for
the firste which is the Giftes of those Eclesiasticall Liveings, if
hee doe not Dispose them to worthy And orthodox Preachers,
they may doe your Majestie much mischeefe, By Abusing your
People the second is, if hee doe not make such Gentle men
Justices of the peace, as are very Loyall, understanding men, &
well sett for your Majesties Goverment, they May doe more
hurte then the ministers, I speake of itt to your Majestie
knowing that these two were very greate Causes of the Late
distempers, Now for the Judges & all Places Judicatture what
soever, I know your Majesties wisedome such as you will Chuse
the ableste, suffitienteste, & honestest Men, And not to follow
the fation of france, to sell places of Judicature, for hee that
byes, will & muste sell, & There Comes In moste horid Coruption, I know your Majestie will not sell them, butt those that
are neere you will, Have a feeling of itt, Itt Should bee lookte
for for the moste Parte they that Speake very Earnestly for
such a man, or so, Hee may bee suspected to have some thing,
or a Large promis, For Comonly Courtiers are not so good
natured, & so Earneste For nothinge, but onely for your
Majesties Service, I Doubte that These Judges then, when they
are returned for their Severall sircutts, aught to give your
Majestie A Juste accounte of all the Serverall Counties, they
have been In, the Dispotition of the people, of greater, or Less
Condition, whoe rules in Every Countye moste, & hath moste
power, & whoe able to Serve your Majestie beste, whoe Loyall
& whoe mutteners, as also the riches of the Countye, & what
trade, & how itt Rises, so of the Corporations, & principall
townes, & how they are sett To Loyallty, So our Majestie will
know beste how to Governe By Imploying those that are the

fitteste to serve your Corecting Justly the Bill that is given your
Majestie for the Pricking of Shreeves, which office is of great
power, these Judges may bee partial, & give your Majestie false
Intelegence, In some perticuler, but in the Generall Sertenly
itt will Hold good, but there is nothing can meet, with Every
thing, But the beste that can bee Done, that your Majestie may
bee Deceeved the Leaste, A Cruel Hard harted Judge to sitt on
Life and Death, for Murderers, Roberes, & petty theeves, and
the Reste, for I have hard of two Judges, one was mercyfull,
And the other Justly to Execute the Lawes, Att the firste the
severe Judge Condemnd many repriveing non & there were
many fewer, Hangd in the mercifull, Judges sercute, But
within two Asisses, the stricte Judge, had not one hangd, For
the theeves ran all into the mercifull Judges sircuitt, so the
stricte Judge proved the more mercifull att Length, when the
mercifull Judge was hanging his Dozen Every sises, so that I
have hard that all the people, prayd for the stricte Judge, when
they Curste the mercifull one, Judges Should never goe any
Circuitt in their owne Country, for feare of partiallety, but I
thinke there Is a Lawe againeste itt, one thing I humbly offer
to your Majestie which is often a ruine to many famellys, & that
is Those that are made shreeves, are att such Huge & vaste
Expences, with a bundance of servants, with rich Clokes,
Sutes, & feathers, & trumpetters, with great feasting of The
Judges, & the Counsellors att Lawe, as they Doe not Recover itt
in many yeares, if not Ruined, both they, & Their Children
with itt, And no Advantage to your Majestie In the world,
Some say the Judges would Looke a wry of them Iff they Did
not so, onely for their Glorry, & pompe, But sertenly the
Judges are both wiser, & more Honorable persons Therefore
your Majestie should doe a moste Gracious worke In publish-
ing your Royall will & pleasure, in Every County For the
moderation, of the Shreeves Expences, to shew your great
care of your Gentery, to Ease them all the ways that Posibly you
Could, which would Infenitly please Them, There was one
Shreeve I hard of that mett the Judges, only with his Clarke,
with a pen & Inke horne Att his Girdle, & told the Judges, that
the office of the High Shreeve, was to see the Judges safely
Conducted Into the County, & safely out of the County, & if
hee did Nott performe that, with his Clarkes pen, & Inke
horne, Then Lett him bee Damed, for by his fayth hee sayd

Hee would not undoe, himselfe, his wife, & Childerne, For the Glorry of the Shreeve, or for the Pompe of the Judges, & In my opinion hee both sayd, & did very wisely.

Now some sayes that your Majestie aught Nott to sitt in any Courte of Justice, which is very Rediculous, & false for your Majestie is the prime & great Judge And makes all the other under you, as all writts is In your Majesties Name, & many kinges uppon severall occations, have sitt In all the Courtes in westminster Hall, though I should Nott advice your Majestie to Doe itt often, for no Judges butt Displeaseth halfe that Comes, before him, Lett him bee Never So Juste, mens partialleties to them Selves are So great, if they have the worste, but they will mutter, Therefore your Majesties wisedome I know will shune that, And put the Displeaseing parte still uppon your Servants, And keepe the pleaseing & mercifull parte still, for your Majestie to Doe, which will Infenitly please your people, with A Duety full affection, & Love to you,—but if you doe Sitt in any Courte, only to Exsamine, the Aparent coruption of Some Judges, & putt them outt, which acte will gaine your Majestie Much Love, There is one thing that hath been a great Mistake In the Gentry, & that was with their Litle tinsell Pride, that they Scornd to bee of Jueries, but to bee a Justice of the peace, or a Debuty Leuftenant, with a Hawke, & a Hound, And then all was well, not Seeing by this meanes, they Loste the power of the kindgome, & putt itt into the hands of the Comons which hath been our bane, for heretofore the beste knights And Gentlemen in the Counties used to bee of Juries, And what is the power of a Juery, itt is this, they have power over all mens personall Estates, Lands, & Liveings, Excepte The Lives of Lords, but for their Estates, they have, & all this is putt into the hands of the Comons, by the pride of the Gentry, it were well, if itt Could bee recovered into the hands of the Gentery agen, which your Majestie may Doe by Comanding the Judges To see itt executed,—which will bee great advantage to your Majestie, for there is no Gentle man, but hath a neerer dependance of your Majestie, then the free holders have, & so More att your Comand,—Now your Majestie knows there is Distributive Justice, & Comutative Justice,—Distributive Justice is only in your Majestie, to reward those, that have Deserved beste, both for their Loyallty, fidelety, Service, And sufferings, which your Majestie is beste Judge of, & only

Judge, For Comutative Justice, that is only betwixte partye &
partye, & where your Majestie I am sure will see Justice, &
right done, unto your Subiects, with our hindering the pro-
sedinges of ordinary Justice, by messages to any Judge by the
Intersesion, off anye Now your Majestie will give mee Leeve to
End with what I did Begin withall,—And that is how to Deminish the superfluty of those that belong to the Lawe,—As
the Phititians Say Take away the Cause, & the Effects will
follow,—So take Such a Course, as to Deminish Sutes, & there
will bee fewer Lawyers, & I know of nothing better then this
that followes

> To have A Regester Generall in Every
> Countye, for the Entery of all Deeds, and
> Convayances, of Land, between party,
> And party, An office of Record,—
>   The Benefitt is This—

That whoe soever sells, or Byes, by this meanes hee Shall see
clearly, what Intrest, & title, is in any land, Hee shall purchase,—where by hee Shall bee assured, that the sale to him is
good,—& thereby will avoyd All future sutes touching the title
of his purchase, & so Bee it greate Ease to the Subiecte, by
avoyding a multeplisety of Sutes————————————
Itt will bee hard to Confirme this by an acte of parlement because there are still so many Lawyeres of the house of Comons,
which will opose itt, because itt hinders the Multeplisety of
Sutes, which is their Gayne, ————————————
This would bee agreat Ease to the subiecte, & add something
To your Majesties Revenues to ————————————
Then the Limitation of a twelve month, from the beginning of
the sute, the sute to bee heard, & Determind, which would bee
agreat Ease to the subiecte,—which the Lawyeres will opose to
for their Gayne ————————————————————
A Resonable Consideration to bee had of all fees, to officers, &
Lawyeres, which would very much Ease the subiecte sertenly,
the Lawyeres will opose this to ————————————
Now some that would play the Polititian, will tell your Majestie
that the more your people are troubled a boute their privat, &
Perticuler affayres, the Less they will thinke of Rebellion, or
Muteneys, which is very false,—for itt teaches them to muteney, And to wrangle,—besides when, or where, was there
more Letigius Sutes, then before these late, & unhappy times,

& sertenly itt Taught them, being so full of the Lawe, to Dispute Every thing, Even the kinges Prerogative, but your Majesties wisedome, will nott Bee abused, by a Logitian, & an orator, that forces Arguments To mentayne falsehoods,— And thus much for the Lawe ————————————————

For the Civill
Lawe

The Arches, & Doctors Comons, is Properly Conserning wills, mariges, furnecation, & Adultery, & many such like things, the coruption hath been greate, in this courte, that Both hath been condemnd for itt, & might have been & have Growne to great Riches,—Therefore I Should humbly advice your Majestie to have the Arch Bishopp of Canterbury, & Bishopp of London, to bee of the High Comition, as I thinke formerly They were,—& so some other Lords of your Majesties privie Counsell, as I am sure the late Earle of Dorsett was one, whoe was a very stricte person, againest all Incontiencey,—These would keepe that Courte, in some reasonable order, for Itt is an Excellent Courte, if itt bee nott a bused, & goe to High, which the Exlesiasticks will strive to make, when the Courte was put Downe, they were forcet to make Comities in The place of itt, which was much worse,—The truth is this Courte, is not so much the Civill Lawe, as the Comon Lawe, which was the popes Lawe,—your majesties courte of Admiralty, is more the Civill Lawe,—& a great advantage, to your Majestie in time of warr, & No smale profitt to yout Masjesties Admirall, Indeed one of the Greatest places that is, now when your Majestie sees what great Profitable offices there are, I should wish as one Did in Henery the Eyghts time, the kinge being poore, though hee had more Riches Lefte him, then Ever any kinge of England had,—so hee wisht the king had a good office, & then hee would be rich ————————————

Ile only tell your Majestie what Tobye Mathew, the Arch Bishope of yorke Sayd, which was this, Sayes his Grace, there was one Saye, that ther was non Less Pious, then Devines, non

Less Juste then Lawyeres,—Non Less Chaste then Cevillians,
—& Non Less temperatt then Phititians,—butt Sayes his Grace
Hee was a knave that Sayd so, butt truely iff for the moste
Parte if itt bee so, the old proverb is verefied, in them, which Is,
That familiarety breds Contempt,

Your Majestie hath great advantage In your Goverment, In
haveing The Church of England wholey to depend uppon
your, being Both king, & pope, nexte & Imediatly after
Christe—Supreme head & Governor,————The Like advantage your Majestie hath in haveing the whole Lawe to Depend uppon you, both Civill, & Comon, yett these two should
Bee kepte, within the modeste bounds, of their own Circles, &
not To swell beyond them, for they prove Diseases then, & not
health For your Majesties Goverment, & the Comon wealth,
—some will saye—They both strive for Dominion, & Govermente, as your Majestie is To Doe nothing againeste the word
of God, which is very true,—butt They will expound Gods will
to bee what is best for their Advantage, & then they are kinges,
& Rule,—The Lawyeres sayes The kinge is to bee obayd, butt
not againeste the Lawe,—& the—Lawyeres will Expound the
Lawe to their beste advantage to Rule—& thus Robb your
Majestie of your subiects, to bee their Subiects, which two
thinges have been great Causes, both of makeing & Continu-
ing this Late rebellion,—but yett I muste tell your Majestie
That the Church of England, was Inosent in this, & did all
They Could to serve you,—Butt the Puretans, & sismatickes
did Fomente the Rebellion, by their preaching of itt perpetually As the people—for the Lawyeres Lett him Answere for
himselfe, Butt itt is very true, that the Lawe & the Gospell,
being kepte within their owne modeste Circles, & bounds,
both depending uppon your Majestie as they aught, I say the
Lawe, & Gospell—Bound upp under your Majesties prerogative, is a great advantage to your Majesties Govermente, In
makeing the subiecte moste happy under your Crowne &
Septer,—Butt this will nott, nor cannott, Confirme your Majestie In a setled Throwne, without your Power, which Is
Armes, for itt is not Devines, preaching Hell, & Damnation, or
Excomunication, that can keepe a company of Rude people,
From throwing him out of the Pulpitt, for without the power
of Armes, the prentices of a shrove tusday, would teare the
Bishopps Moste Reverent Lawne Sleeves, from his Armes, &

cutt his throte to Boote,—Neyther is itt a writte with a litle yallow wax, that Can secuer the Lawyere, or the Judges Scarlett Gowne, his tipp stafe, Mace, or Cryer, no sr. itt is Armes, which is your Juste power, That keepes peace, in the Church, & Justice in the Lawe, & but For that power your Majestie might bee driven from white Hall,—Tis nott Logicke, & oratory, serves the turne againest Multetudes, witnes this Late horid rebellion, which they Could never Doe until they Gott the Armes into their hands, And I know your Majestie is to wise, to bee persuaded to the contrary By Gowne, men, whose perpetuall ambition is to Governe, And they are so afrayd of Armes, that mentaynes their vocations, as they would rather venter an other Rebellion Then to have them,—I wonder what all the Learning of the universeties did, or doe againest the Redd Coates,—what Did all the sages of the Lawe, doe againeste the Redd Coates & what doth the History of Pompe, & Cesar, doe any good Againeste Cromwell, or any record frome william the Conqueror, doe againeste Cromwell,—no Sr. your power is nothing but Armes, For without them nothing will bee obayd, but att their Pleasure, & there fore Looke to the foundation, which is that To Establish your Majestie—Safe in your throwne, your subiectes In their Juste Rights, the Church In peace, & the Lawe to bee free, that the Judges may administer Justice, And the whole peace of the kingdome never to feare by this Meanes, a Civill warr, but that Every man thus will Pray for your Majestie & bless your happy Goverment,—Since Every subiecte thus may sitt safe under his owne vine, And not feare the Distruction of the whole kingdome, by A Civill warr.

For Trade

Your Majestie will bee pleased to Consider, that Trade is an other Busines, then the Church, or the Lawe, for those two Laste Robbs The Hive of the Comon wealth, of their Honye but bringes Non to the Hive,—No sr. itt is the merchant, that only brings Honye to the Hive,—itt is hee only that in riches kingdomes By trade, & Espetially your Majesties kingdome of

Englnd, that is ordained for itt, itt is not an ill winter, that the Country man Complaynes on, that makes scarsetye of monye, but the Decay of Trade,—for itt is a sertene Rule, that never fayles, when Every thing is Cheape, there is a scarsety of money, when Every thing is deare, then the kingdome is full of money,—for Exsample Imagine all the Comon wealth In 4 or 5 persons And they to have butt five pound a peece,—& a sixt person Is to sell them a horse, & that sixt person is nesesetated To sell him,—why then hee muste sell him for five pound For no more, hath any more to give, & hee can have no More then there is, but put the Case these five persons Had a £100 a peece, why then this sixt man that is to sell His horse, may have a £100 for him, because those 5 persons Hath a £100 a peece, & may give itt, Thus your Majestie sees that Plenty of money, makes Every thinge Deere, & scarsety of Money of nesesety muste make Every thing cheape, therefore your Majestie will bee pleased to keepe upp the merchant, that can only fill your kingdome with riches, & so Consequently inrich your Majestie for if your kingdome bee poore, where can your Majestie Have itt, no where, therefore your Majestie will bee pleased to Inrich your kingdome, that neyther your Majestie nor your subiects May wante, & that is Done absolutly by the merchant, & only By the merchant, which to boote Increases a Bundantly your shipping, & so Consequently mareners, which is the greatest Advantage your Majestie Can have, both to make you rich, & powerfull at home, & a terror to all your great Neyghbors abroad for itt is The sea: that terefies, & masters the Land, & makes great Kinges, if not your subiects, yett subiecte to you, & muste subiecte them selves unto your will,—Therefore your Majestie will bee pleased to keepe upp the merchant, as High as posibly you can, so your Majestie bee master of them, that is to be master of London, & the River, & then no body can bee, to Rich, butt itt will bee founde a great benefitt both to your Majestie & the Comon wealth, trade muste bee Considered, that The marchant may Exporte more then Importe, that hee Carry out more Comodieties, then hee brings In, that is That hee sell more, then hee byes, & then itt is moste sertene That the kingdome muste bee full of money, the staple Comodaties of the kingdome, as Lead, Iron, Tin, Cloth, & many More Comodeties of Great valewe,—Itt is trad & trafficke That fills the kingdome, with money,—itt is not setting Higher valewes uppon money, than doth any good, or debaseing of itt, Those are butt shiftes, for present turnes, & Doth much Hurte afterwarde, besides the discreditt of itt, & non butt Poore, & nesesatated prince, will Doe itt, & wise princes will never Doe itt, because they will never bee poore, & Putt the Case a twenty shilling Peece were raysed to 30S, And an other forayne prince, will rayse itt to 40S, & so vie itt, And see it, Eternally, whats gott by this,—no tis Trade—That bringes In Gold, & silver, for Lett a forrayne prince Make a twenty shilling peece, five pounde, keepe upp the merchant, And I dare undertake, the Gold, & Silver, shall follow the Trade into England, therefore that is the business, & the mayne busines, to keep upp trade, which is the merchant, The more merchantdise doth—Increase, the more is your Majesties Coustums, which non Grudeges att, Butt moste willing, to pay them, being so well ordered, as nott To pull Downe trade, butt kept in that measure as to Increase trade, & fills your Majesties Coffers, but truely I have Heard, that there hath been Great a buse by the farmers of the Coustam house, some getting £20000 a yeare, some 15,000, And some 12,000 at the leaste, & lived Like Emperors, when the Kinge was forcet continually to borrow,—this should bee Dilligently lookte into,—for itt Consernes your Majestie very much, There is non repines att your Majesties Coustums, but att monopoles Extreamely, & they have great reson, as the moste Distructive Thinge to the Comon wealth, in the world, & there non hath More reson to Complayne of itt, then your Majestie for Litle Comes to your share sr. butt to privatt purses, & so your Majestie is More Cozened then the Comon wealth,—& to a bolish all Those monopoles Even by Proclemation would Cry your Majestie upp a father of the Comon wealth, without much Loss to your Majestie, butt greate gayne in the End, for Sertenly the Subiecte would bee so well pleased with itt, as uppon any occation They woulde off upp their purses to your Majestie,—I have Heard much Discourse of free trade, what great—Advantage that would bee to the Comon wealth, I have Heard much of this Discourse, both In Parlements, & out of Parlement, disputed hottly, both pro: & con:, & By merchants, that is, London merchants, & merchants of other porte Townes, thinkeing London devored the Trade of all other Townes, but I could never heare itt well resolved, I am sure,

never setled, Nay the merchants oposeres to London, says that
their Companys are monopoles Againeste free trade,—As the
Turkey Companey, the Hamborow Company, & Easte Indea
Company,—I am not so well reade In trade, as to Determine
the poynte,—but Indeed for the Easte Indea Company, ther
may be something sayd unto that, for they say they Carry
many hundereth Thousande poundes In spetie, in Silver, out
of the kingdome that should bee Lookte to, Indeed,—butt I
knowe nott what they Can say for them selves, I have heard
when itt was questiond, They used strong Arguments of the
purse, to Great persons, To Continue their trade,—Butt sayes
some, How shall the Kinge keepe upp the merchant, marry as
his Majesties Coustomes, Are Gentle, itt Incourages to trade,
for if itt were otherwise, The merchants would Leave tradinge,
when they saw they Could not Gayne by itt, & then the
Coustomes would be nothing, Butt this is nott all, your Majestie to supporte them against any Prince in the world, that
Durste offer them Iniuries, as when Their goods are taken, or
seased on any wayes, your Majestie Eyther To take, or give
them Leave to take twice as much of theirs, And then Dispute
itt,—but I doe not love a Disputation with The Loss, thraten a
warr to your neyghbors, if they Doe not doe your Subiects
right, Give Letters of marte, & all the wayes to suporte the
merchant that posibly your Majestie can, & your Majestie will
Finde both much Honor, & profitt by itt, for your Majestie
needs Feare, neyther france, or spayne, & to satisfie Eyther of
their Embasadors, that are butt spies, uppon your Majestie &
your kingdomes, To pleasure them, againeste your merchants, I see no reson for Itt, att all, but if they take twice as
much from them, And then Dispute itt, so to help your Merchants, with your Majesties Shipps for Convoyes, & gardes to
them, your Majestie alwayes haveing Shipps for the Garde of
your Coaste, to Doe itt, without any Charge to you, & this is the
protection, & keeping upp of the merchante, your Majestie
will please to give mee leave, to Deliver my opinion, which is
this,—that itt is Imposible, for any man, to bee A good
states-man that doth not understand trade In some Measure,
which I will shew your Majestie by what fell outt In Queen
Elizabeths Rayne,—The king of spayne, made great Prepera-
tions both by Sea, & Land,—so that old Burley—Secretary
Walsingam, Lester, & Earle of Sussex, which were no Fooles,

butt very wise Counsellors, Concluded by all their Intelegence
that this great preperation, of the king of spayne by all prob-
abilety was againeste England, to Doe no thinge, they mighte
bee surprised, And to make a suffiente resistance would bee
such a vaste charg, Her Majisties Coffers being not full, as they
knew not how to turne themselves, or what to doe,—so att
Laste a greate & Rich Citizen of London, one Sr. Thomas
Gressham, a famous person for building the old Exchange att
London, by the moddell of the Exchange at Antwerpe, Besides hee built Gressham Colledge, & In dowed itt, with good
Revenues, for many usefull, & Excellent Lectors,—This sr
Thomas Gressham heareing how the Queen, & her Counsell
were pusled A boute this great affayre, goes to the Courte, &
Desired that hee Might wayte of her Majestie, & such Counsellors to bee by, as shee Pleased to make Choyce of, & so shee
did, & there sr Thomas Gressham undertooke, with a smale
Charge in Comparison of a great Fleete, or a land Army, to
assure her Majestie, that the king of Spayne should doe her no
hurte, that yeare,—the Queen askte Him how, & hee told her
Majestie that the king of Spayne Could Nott doe itt without
money, & hee knew the king of spayne Muste Borrow that
money to of merchants, so that hee Could prevent him, both
att Antwerp, Genoa, venise, & att Hamborow, for Amsterdam
was nothing then, that hee would take upp such great sums, as
the king of spayne should Have no money, & so stopp his
Designe, & itt was but Paying so much Intreste, for a few
months, which was an Inconsiderable sum, In Comparison of
a preparation Eyther By Sea, or Land, the Queen & her
Counsell was over Joyed with the proportition, gave him great
thankes, toke his Counsell, & did absolutly stopp the king of
spaynes Designes, That year, that hee Could doe nothing, & so
had roome To turne them, with time, for the nexte yeare,
—And now your Majestie sees what adavantage the understanding of Trade is for a states Man,—one word of Impotitions, & monopolies,—Impotitions Comes to your Majesties
purse, & hinders not trade, or tradsmen, Butt they are as they
were beefore, only paying so much, which uppon the poynte,
Every subiecte payes for itt, being the Comodety, So itt Lights
Generally uppon the subiecte, & not uppon the Tradsmen,
because they Hoyse upp their Comodeties accordingly, Butt
monopoles is a moste Horible thing, both to your Majestie

haveing Butt a Smale Sum God knowes, & heere one perticuller man Ingroses all the trade of that Comodetie, to himselfe, or his owne use, not suffering any man to trade Excepte hee will Compound with him, & att his owne rates, & by that meanes many a Trades man Breakes, & is undone, both hee, & his wife, And Childeren, as they did in the monopoley of Sope, & many others,—& all for Some perticuller men, which your Majestie Had much better that they were Hanged, then so many Famellyes undone, & those that mayntayne the kingdome, Then those that Destroy itt,—for taxes Even parlement Subsedies,* fiveteenes are very unJustly Layd, as for Exsample the Subsedies In your Majesties Royall Auncesters times, were as much A gen, then, as they are now, though money was Scarse then, And plentyfull now, for then as I take itt, a subsedie was a 120000 & now it is but 60000 which is but halfe, —The reson is that the beste men in the Countye, are still made Comitioners for the subsedye, & though their Grand fathers Payd £60 they pay not £30 the reson is they pull Downe one Another, since they can sease as they please, & laye itt on the poorer sorte, & so itt Comes Shorte halfe, so that when your Majestie, thinkes you have a great matter, In so many Subsedies you have nott halfe what your Royall predesesors had,—A greate A buse, & Comes this way that I tell your Majestie of—Indeed—There is no taxe or sesment, that is Equall,—neyther by the Muster Booke, or the booke of Rates, that which is absolutly the Moste Equall, is the Exsise,—for there no man pays for more—Then hee hath,—all the advantage is, that a rich Curmougion That will almoste starve himselfe, with raw porke, & Candles Endes, may have advantage for the purse, though not the belly,—Butt that Cannot bee helpte, but how a parlement will Like of an Exsise, I know nott,-This digression from trade I aske pardon for, though itt Comes not Impertinently In Neyther,—for Corporations I see no reson why there should Bee so many, for why should Taners, & Shooe makers, not bee Contented, to bee Governed by the same way, that Lords, gentlemen And good yeomen, & freeholders are, which is by the knowne Lawes of the kingdome, by the Judges & Justices of peace, But these Townes-

---

*Subsedies uppon lande, fiveteens uppon goods, by the poll perticuler persons.

men muste bee Exsempted by their Chartter, the Truth is, that
Every Corporation, is a petty free state, Againest monarkey, &
they have Done your Majestie more mischeefe, In these late
disorders, with their Lecturers, then anything Else hath done,
therefore your Majestie will bee pleased to Thinke of itt, for all
their Charters, are forfitted, itt were good to have some Considerable Townes, that are Built much uppon trade, but nott
so many—Itt is A mighty Riches that belonges to Corporated
Townes, In land, that they have bought, which some way is to
No porpose, but to make so many, feastes, to bee drunke so
many times a yeare, & spend so many brace of Buckes, And
thats all, the good of itt, what soever they pretend, sayes some
but itt is their owne, & they may use itt As they please,—I
should Humbley advice that your Majestie would bee pleased
to Increase manufactor all that Posibley Could bee, all over
your kingdome, as makeing all severall Maner of stuffes, as the
duch-men doe att Norwich, so silke stuffes, Cloth of Gold, &
silver, as they doe att Genoa, & Millan, silke wormes itt may bee
will finde England to Cold for them, butt itt were well, it should
bee tryed, & mulberry Tree sett for their foode, butt if this
fayle Rawe silkes, & to bee wraught upp in England,—makeing of linen Cloth of all sortes, as Hollands, deemy Holland,
Cambricks, Lawne, & for which much fine flaxe is to be sowed
so For all maner of fine threed Laces, as Flanders is famous For
itt, Iper and Gante hath been famous Above 300 yeares For
Chaser speakes of itt—Butt some will say this may Hinder
trade, what hindering of trade doth itt in Flanders & Brabante,
is itt not as good, to gett money For these Comodities, as to give
money for these Comodeties, yes, & much better, sertenly, for
one doth inrich the kingdome, & the other doth Impoverish
itt,—Butt if itt were for nothing Else, butt to sett your subiects
a worke, both male, & female, not only to busie them, but that
by their Labor they might live, & many grow rich without being A Burthen to the Comon wealth, which will bee a mighty
advantage both for your Majesties Govermente, & for the
peace of the kingdome, which otherwise by poverty, & Idlenes,
might Produce many Inconvencies, both to your Majestie &
your kingdome, because moste Things in this world is governed by the price of money, for when money was at ten in the
hundereth, then Lands was att fiveteen yeares purchase, when
it came down to Eyght in the hundereth, this Land was at

twenty yeares purchase, now being at six in the hundereth, Land is at five & twenty yeares purchase,—so if your Majestie brings itt To Eyght agen, it is a good propotion, & will make forrayners Espetialy Hollanders, where money goes so low to bring all their money, for that profitt into England, & so fill your Majesties kingdome full of money which Lately they have taken away, being but att six in the hundereth.

For the Countery

To bee Governd by Judges In all the severall Counties, by the Asises twice a yeare, sheriffes & good Justices of peace at their Quarter Sessions, & those Justices, to bee well Chosen, to bee Loyally disposed, with their severall officers, as Cheefe Constables Petty Counstables headborrows & the like,—with Justices of the Coram, & Ratulorum,—butt the mayne busines Is a troupe of Horse In Every Countie, & some Dragoners in Every County Proportionable to the Countye, more, or Less, & to bee removed To severall parts of the County, as occation Serves, & the Dragoners when they are not horste they are musketters, & then I woulde Have some of them Pikes, to bee a garde for the Magazens In Every County,—the Tropers I would have Gentlemens Younger Sonns, to tye their fathers, & Brothers more to your Majestie, and one thing I desire your Majestie to take Care of which is never to Lett The country pay the soldier, butt only your Majestie your selfe, for the soldier will follow the mony, & God forbidd the soldeir should have Any Dependance In the world butt uppon your Majestie, for otherwise Itt would bee a very dangerous busines, since force doth all, therefore itt is the greatest conserne, your Majestie can have, to Looke To,—what soever they would give to pay them, by such officers as your Majestie shall appoynt,—no Lord Leuftenante, or trayne bands to Depend on the people, but a Lord Governor of the province, of your Majesties Troopes, the Rebells understands this to well, & hath Done itt to your Hands,—There is one thing that is agreat trouble to the kingdome And is litle Lookte after, & that is sturddy vagarant Roggs—That are beggers throughout the kingdome, itt should bee Lookte unto carefully, there are Excellent Laws, for itt, butt they Are never putt in Exsecution, & then it were as good to have Non, the Correction Houses weare of good use, if they were used As they should bee,—In the states Dominions they are very—Dilegent in this poynte, haveing not a begger of their owne Country that Beggs, butt is provided for by his owne Labor,—As if hee bee Lame, of his feete, they make him worke with his hands, if Lame of his hands, they make him worke with His feete, nay they make blinde people turne wheeles, in severall trades, to gett their Liveinges, & the parish provieds for Non butt old decrepett people, butt what is this to stoute And sturdy rogges, that may worke, & will nott, & doth a world of mischeefe,—this should bee Lookte to,—Judge Denham that was a wise, & a very honest Gentleman, Complaynd Exceedingly of those stoute Rogges,—There is also Companys of Gipseyes that should bee Distroyd, for they are all theeves, To bee a Gipseye Is felloney by the statute Lawe, but that Lawe is never put In Execution, so that the kingdom is full of them,—for dround Landes to bee drand is a great advantage to the Comon wealth, which the Duchmen Did well in,—for before, where there was Nothing but a muddy pike, or a Ducke, now there are A bundance of good sheepe, & fatt oxen, great store of corne, of all kindes, wadd, & Rapeseed which are of great use, & Profitt, wadd for Dyeing, & Rape seed for oyle, for Leather, And such things, therefore your Majestie will Incourage the Drayners All that may bee,—the Country man will Complayne of any thing That is newe,—& so the parlement to please the people was againeste Itt,—but now they have put itt upp agen,—This Distructive, No Goverment, hath done nothing but mischeefiously to Pull Downe, but they have builte nothinge,—so they have distroyd the woodes of England Extreamely, which is an Intolerable Loss, since they are not to bee repeared In many Ages,—but I thinke your Majestie might doe very well, to give order for the sowing of Acorns, & after have them planted in severall—Places, as they doe in Braban, & flanders, which will bee a Great benefitt to after Ages, & a fine shad in a few yeares, Though an oke bee Long before hee Comes to his perfection, For shipping, or building, butt as I take itt there is an Excellent Lawe for that purpose, which if itt bee put in Execution, all Posterety will thank your Majestie for itt,—I should humbley advice your

Majestie to Disaforeste all your forrestes, chases, & parkes,
that are Remote from you, & so of litle use, & Less profitte,
—there—would be much to your Majesties Coffers, firste by
the sale of woodes, nexte For a Compotition with all foresters,
for their owne, Eyther fine, or rente,—& then by the sale of
your Majesties owne Land,—& Nowe you have nothinge butt
a Company of Idle keepers, verderers, wood wordes, stuartes,
& many other officers, that doth nothing—Butt Coosen your
Majestie, In Every thinge, of Every thing,—The Benefitt For
the Comon wealth is great, firste to bee free of the forreste
Lawes, which are very punishable, the nexte they will build
vilages, & Increase those that are, & have abundance of good
corne, where there was nothing but heath before, & where any
Man kepte a Draught before, hee will nowe bee able to Keepe
two, or three, & where there are hundereths of beggers nowe,
that Lives of nothinge, but getting, & selling of billberrys, A
very poore trade, which continues them beggers still,—when
The forrestes are disforrested, the Tillege will bee so greate, as
Itt will sett all the Beggers a worke, Male, & female, for Corne
hath always somethinge, to bee Done aboute itt, Even from the
sowing, to the Reaping, so that truely within A while, in that
place, there will bee almoste no beggers, In so good Estate, will
they bee,—And thus your Majestie—will gayne very much by
itt, & your People to,—Iff they Talke of Increaseing of people,
sertenly Beggers increase More then rich folkes, but should
they, A warre will Emtye them, Eyther by Land, or sea,—or
Else your Majestie May send Colonies, to the bermodies, Vir-
ginia, Barbadoes, New England, & New Scotland, &c. ———

For Seremoney, & Order

Seremoney though itt is nothing in itt Selfe, yett it doth
Every thing,—for what is a king, more than a subiecte, Butt for
seremoney, & order, when that fayles him, hees Ruiend,—
what is the Church, without Seremoney, & order, when that
fayles, the Church is Ruind,—what is the Lawe without Seremoney, & order, when that fayles, the Lawe Goes Downe,

—what are the universeties, & all Scooles, without Seremoney,
& order, nothing, what are all Corporations, without Seremoney, & order, nothing,—what is a Lord more Then a
footman, without Seremoney, & order,—A Dispised Title,
—what is parents, & Childeren, masters, & Servants, officers
in all kindes, in the Comon wealth, without Seremoney, And
order, nothing at all,—Nay what is an Armey without Seremoney, & order, & there the strictest Seremoney, & order, for
hee that Continues Longest in order, which is In Bodyes, wines
the Battle:,—what are all Counsells, & states, without Seremoney, & order, nothing but Confution, & Ruin, So that
Seremoney, & order, with force, Governes all, both In peace,
& warr, & keepes Every man, & Every thing within the Circle
of their owne Conditions,—Nay very Beare Baiting, without
Seremoney, & order, would bee in more Confution then it is,
& many such like things,—therefore your Majestie will bee
pleased to keepe itt upp strickly, in your owne, person, &
Courte, to bee a presedent to the reste of your Nobles, & not to
make your selfe to Cheape, by to much Familiarety, which as
the proverb sayes, breedes Contempte But when you appeare,
to shew your Selfe Gloryously, to your People; Like a God, for
the Holly writt sayes, wee have Calld you Godds—& when the
people sees you thus, they will Downe of their knees, which is
worshipp, & pray for you with trembling Feare, & Love, as
they did to Queen Elizabeth, whose Goverment Is the beste
presedent for Englandes Govermente, absolutly; only these
Horrid times muste make some Litle adition To Sett things
strayght, & so to keepe them,—And the Queen would Say God
bless you my good people,—& though this Saying was no great
matter, in it selfe, yet I assure your Majestie, itt went very farr
with the people,—nay of a Sunday when shee opend the window, the people would Cry, oh Lord I saw her hand, I saw her
hand, & a woman, cryed out oh Lord Sayd shee, the Queens a
woman,—Sertenly there is nothing Keepes upp a king, more
than seremoney, & order, which makes Distance, & this
bringes respecte & Duty, & those obedience which is all,—Nay
hee is a foole that is to bold with your Majestie Even in your bed
chamber, & those that are so, I know your Majesties wisedome
will give them a Checke for itt, & if they Doe not mend, putt
them oute,—& your Majestie will finde much quiett, & benefitt
By itt,—so if your Majestie please to Speake to your Harraldes

to sett Downe, the Seremoney, & order, for all Degrees of your
Nobilety, as For Barrons, viscounts, Earles, Marquises, &
Dukes,—& to have Itt printed,—& so for all the great officers,
their Seremoney, & order,—& not any to Intrench, one uppon
an other, but to keep only what is right, & dewe, for their
places, & Digneties, As one thing, non under the Degree of a
Barronnes, can have Carpetts, by her Bedd, & shee but one, or
two, at the moste And now Every Turkey merchants wife, will
have all her Floore over with Carpetts,—so now Every Citizens
wife will Have six Horses, in her Coach, which is moste un-
fitting, they say The ways are so foule, when tis their pride, for
I am sure when I was A boy, Gilbert the great Earle of
Shrewsbury Never went but with foure Horses in his Coch, &
those of meaner Degrees, butt with two horses, & traveled
many hundered Miles, & the ways as foule as they are now, the
king of spayne alowes No body six Horses but himselfe,—this
your Majestie will rectefie very Easeyly,—so to make no Difference between great Ladys, & Citizens wifes, in aparell is
abhominable,—no they should goe To their Little blacke vel-
vett Cappes, smale Gold Cheanes, & Litle Ruffes, as they were
in my time, & their Aprentices in their Rounde blacke Capps,
but this muste take a litle time, for Feare of offending to faste,
untill your Majestie bee well setled in your Sadle,—& when any
of these orders are violated, to bee brought into the martialls
Courte, & there punisht, which Courte Though itt was spoken
againeste in parlement, is a moste Excellent Courte, for itt
keepes upp seremony, & order, so the Courte bee kepte within
his bounds,-for Sertenly, degrees of Aparell, to Severall Conditions, & callings, is of Great Consequence, to the peace of the
kingdome, for when Lower Degrees strives to out brave
Higher Degrees, itt breeds Envie In the better Sorte, & pride
in the Meaner, Sorte, & a contempt, by the vulger of the
Nobilety,—which breeds Faction, & disorder, which are the
Causes of a Civill warr, Therefore Sire keepe upp your
Nobility, & Gentery, to all their Juste rights & dignities, For
what kepte upp your Royall father so long, but parte of the
Nobility, & Gentery, when hee had no money, which as the
sinews of warr, mayntayneing them selves, & his warr, almoste
att their owne Charge, & held out beyond all Expectation,—itt
was neyther the Church, nor the Lawe, that kepte upp the king
so long, butt parte of the Nobilety, & Gentery, therefore your

Majesties wisdome, will cherish them,—tis true, wise kinges heretofore, tooke as much power from the Nobilety, as they could, because of the Barrons warrs,—& put More to the Comons, wherein they Comitted a very greate Error For the worste in the Nobility is, but to pull downe one king, & sett upp an other, so that they are always for monarkey, butt the Comons, pull downe Roote, & branch, & utterly distroyes monarky, so that your Majestie will bee pleased to sticke to your Nobilety, & gentery, And they will sticke to you, being in no great danger, as long as your Majestie hath the force, in your hands, being denied, into so many hands, of the Nobilety, which is as many Lords, as there are Counties, which is 52: & sertenly all those are not likely to agree at one time againeste you,—In my time, Gilberte that great Earle of Shrewsbury whoe was a wise man, & had a gentle soule, & a Loyall,—at a St. Georges feaste, I have knowne Sir Georg booth a Cheshere knight And of six, or seaven, thousand pound, a yeare, weare my Lord of Shrewsburys blew Coate, on St. Georges Day,—as also Sir Vinsent Corbett, whose brother had 10,000 a yeare, & after the death of His brother, hee had 4 or 5000 a yeare, & hee wore my Lords Blew Coate, of a St. Georges Day also,— butt the nexte day they satt both at my Lords table nexte him, & nothing butt good Coosen Corbett, & good Coosen booth, & they were very wise in itt, for thus they did oblige my Lord, to bee their servant all the yeare After, with his power to serve them, both in Courte, & westminister Hall, & to bee their solister,—& agen my Lord had no busines in the Country, but they did itt for him,—& then the king had an Easey busines, for what soever busines his Majestie had in any County In England, or in all England, itt was but speaking to Shewsbury, or Darby, & such great men, & itt was Done, with Ease & subilety, which a Lawyere with a Comition, would finde Rubbs in, & put your Majestie uppon Extremetyes, to discontent your people, & what doth itt coste your Majestie, a blew Riban, a privey Counsellor shipp, or such offices as your Majestie Cannot bestow better, then uppon such great men, For the people doth not Envey great men, as they doe meaner, men, & then all their kindered, freinds, dependances, servants tenantes, are well pleased, & your Majestie safe,—but now the pride of the times are such, as if very meane men bee not made of your Majesties bedd Chamber,—they presently Rebell, & grow—

discontented, which is such a Rediculous pride,—when In my
time, I knew william Earle of Penbrooke, that moste Excellent
Person, Labor as for his Life, all the Rayne of king James, As
also the Rayne of king Charles, to bee of the Bedd chamber,
And Could never obtayne itt,—as also Thomas the Great Earle
of Arundell, did Labor to bee of the bedd chamber; Both those
Raynes & could never obtayne itt,—Therefore These meane
fellows are brave presumptious Creatures, that dares offer att
Itt, & then bee disconted forsooth because theye are Justly
Denied,—itt was a Comon thing at Courte to have Ladyes, &
Countises to Laught, at Seremoney & order, in Subiectes,
saying the king, & Queen, could have no more, thinking Thus
to flatter Majestie, & the other reson was, because there were
so many buggerly people, made great Lords, & Ladys, in
Title—That were not able to keep upp the Dignety, of itt, & so
they would Jeere at that, they Could not doe, but what became
of itt, when the Seremoney, & order, of Noble-men were
puled—Downe, which is the foundation of monarkey,—monarkey soone After fell,—for it is a rediculous thing, for any to
thinke so Much seremoney, takes of from a king, butt addes
much to him, For when a Noble man hath so much Seremoney
done unto him, whate doth the people thinke the king is, when
they see this Noble man Sarve as Cupbearer of his knees, or
Suer, or Carver, uppon great days or uppon any day to kiss His
hand, uppon his knee, or kneele to him, whilste his Majestie Is
Sitting, Sertenly sire this addes much to you, & gives Magisty A
great Luster,—when Hayle fellow well mett takes much off of
your Majesties dignetye,—therefore sire keepe upp your
Nobiletye for your own Sake,—There was a prety way they
had att Courte, that meane people that were aboute the king,
& the Queen, would Jeere the Greatest Noble man in England,
Iff hee did not make the Laste months Reverance, a La mode,
that came with the Laste Dancer, from Paris, packt upp in his
fidle Case, & no matter of Regarde of the Nobilety at All, but
some few to Monopolise the king, & the Queen totalye to
Themselfes, this did Infinitly Discontent the Nobilety, & Gentery, & one of the thinges that braught these woefull times,
uppon us, to make much of meane men, that had neyther—
partes, or power, & to neclecte those that had both partes, &
Power, those men to bee respected, that could not rayse A
man, but only lied of the king, & the others that Lived of

Themselves, & could rayse thousands, to bee Dispised, because they did not make Le bon Reverance, & could not Dance a Sereban with castenetts of their fingers,—but your Majesties wisdome will take an other course, & courte your Nobilety, & gentery, & Discourse with them & Cale them to you & cherishe them for they deserve itt.

The Errors Off State, & Their Remedies

The Greateste Error, in these Laste two Raynes were that The kinges alwayes wanted money, which is the Greatest Error—A king can make, wether itt were profusnes, In Giftes or In unnesarye thinges, as pictures, juells, or the Like, or Coosend, but sertenly wante in a king, at Laste Comes to Ruine, —for being Nesesetated, putts him uppon many Ilegall taxes which much offends The People, & then the nexte Parlement is Inflamed, & the king Forcte to Remedy them, to give Contentment to his people, And so goes Less in his subiectes opinions, & makes the very Clownes see that a parlement can order him, & so may thinke that A Parlement hath the trancsendent Power, which itt hath Nott,—butt farr from itt,— Nay should non of these taxes bee, Butt that your Nesesetyes did urge you to Call a parlemente,—That Parlement would thinke they had your Majestie on the Hipp & would play uppon you accordingly, for they would give you no Money untill they had what they desired, & this cannot bee A free Parlemente, for they would bargin with you, & play uppon your nesesety, & have ten times the worth of what they bye, very Much to your Preiudice,—therefore as the old saying is, putt money in your purse, & keepe itt,—Henery the Sevanth your Royall Ancester was a wise king, & hee did so, & would offten say that England was a good farme, if itt were well husbanded, & his Majestie was the Beste husband of itt, that Ever I heard off, & therefore was not Putt to such plunges, as nesesetated princes are,—A Spairing Prince, is good for himselfe, & his people, but not Courtiers, which are but a few in Comparison of the reste, when you are rich, your greate neyghbores, will

feare you to, which if you bee poore, They will not Care for
you,—when you are rich & call a parlement your Majestie is
then master of the feilde, & you may doe what you Please, &
then they have no ground to worke of againeste you, oh riches
sire in a king is more advantages both at home & A Broad then
I can Express, therefore sire Putt money in your Purse & bee
rich,—There is nothing better then To Governe by well Regulated Parlements,—And if your Majestie Bee not nesesetated, but rich, they will bee Regular, parlements. Should bee
kepte within their bounds,—which Every body knows,—For
your Majestie gives Life or death to bills that Pass both houses,
For itt is no Lawe without you sire—& if they give you butt few
Subsedies, pass their resonable Lawes, & give them their—
Subsedies agen, with many good words & thanks, as Queen
Elizabeth Did, for never any had parlements att her will so
much, as shee, Because shee was not nesesatated, so I will End
with this agen, Bee Rich, which is a very Easey thing for you, &
your Majestie will Finde the Greate Benefitt & Sweet of itt, —

The next Error was makeing so many Lordes, which made
the upper House, more factious then the Lower, House, nay
the house of Comons Had not been factius butt for them, for
as soone as Ever one Is made a Lord, hee thinkes himselfe
then, capable of the greateste Place in England, though moste
unfitt, partialety, hath—such force, & if hee bee Denied then
hee growes factius, & makes Parties, & Joynes with the house
of Comons, to Disturb your Majesties Goverment,—Queen
Elizabeth found the sweet, of a few Lords, I thinke shee made
not a bove three Earles, in all her time, Essex, Lincolne, &
Nottingame, & very few barrons,—then the House was so thin
of Lords, as old Burleghie when hee stood upp To Deliver a
message from the Queen, Every Lord stood upp with His
modeste content, & satt him downe agen, there was no Faction, there was no Joyneing, with the house of Comons, in
these Days, neyther the house of Comons any faction in itt, &
all by the multeplisety of Lords, that hath made this faction, &
Those factous a purpose to bee Lords, soe that the fewer
Lordes The Less faction, & Espetialy if those Lords bee not
nesesetated so that your Majestie will be pleased to bee spare-
ing in makeing Lords, For your owne sake, but Lett them die
outt, & make few more, And those that are made, to bee sure
they have meanes, to supporte itt, or Else you rayse faction

againest you, & Envey in Those that are not made, Lordes that thinkes themselves as Good men Every way,—nay some have been made Lords they say That have not a bove £300 a yeare which was a strong thing. An other Error was, that factions att Courte were not Suppreste, for beleeve mee sire all the great mischeefe In Parlements Came out of the kinges house, for the weaker faction In Courte, Did strive always to pull downe the stronger, by a parlemente, where they did not only make their freinds & Servants of the house to doe what they could, to packe A Parlemente, but also did poysen the Country, Gentlemen with severall stories, againeste your great officers, & favoritts, And did flatter & Insineuatt but to farr, to abuse those Honeste Country Gentle men, & when they had served their Turnes of them, then they sent them home to hunt & hauke, A gen, This is to great a knowne truth,—& when they were mett, then they had privat meetings, & continuall Intilegence From these courtiers, from time, to time, what to doe, —An other Error to suffer Parlements to pull downe men att their pleasure, & teare them from your sides wether you will or no, A thing of moste Dangerous Consequence, to your Majestie for when they have found the tricke of itt, they will goe higher Even to the king, as wee have found by woefull Experience, when My Lord St. Albanes, & Earle of Midlesex were prosecuted by the Parlement, I have hard that your Majesties Royall father, & the Late Duke of Buckingam, desired your Majesties Royall Grandfather, king James, to Condesend to the parlement, which muste bee to the Ruine of those two Lordes, for Ragione del Stato,—& king James puld outt his handcercheefe & wepte, & sayd, I doe not weepe For these two Lords, butt for you two, for after they are Hartend or Hooded with this, Buckingam you will bee the nexte, And then Charles will follow, & God knowes itt was to true A Prophysey, but hee was afore seeing wise kinge.—what A strang thing was itt, of the Earle of strafford, Litle or nothing Againeste him, & yett hee muste bee Exsecuted, butt my Lord of Canterbury nothing in the world, againeste him, yett hee muste dye, & nothing so Horid or Insufferable as for a man to bee accused of high Treson as the Bishopp of Canterbury was and Comitted & nothing Could bee Layd to his Charge,—moste unjust, & againeste the petition of Right, & Liberty of the Subiecte,—— But this was a rebellious pacte trayterly Company, And not a parlement, there is nothing better to Governe by, Eyther for

your Majestie or your people, & I hope to see the Blessing of
you & Itt, & your Majestie the blesedeste monarke, that Ever
was in our kingdomes,—butt if the king had been rich this had
not been, or fewer Lords, & for punishing great persons by
Parlement, your Majestie muste keepe that prerogative to
your selfe, And only to your selfe, or Else itt will bee much
worse for your Majestie And if they bee faulty to your Majestie,
or to the Comon wealth, doe Punish them, & to the purpose,
but keepe the Power of punishmente only In your Selfe,
—————There may bee good Lawes made, but Moste thinke
there are to many already for the Subiects, for if wee lived not
under a gracious king, the Penall statutes, were They putt in
Exsecution, would undoe all your subiects, being trapes Rather then helpes to them, as many wise men have thought, But
good kinges never takes advantage of them, which is more
Their Gracious favor, then our fathers, & our Considerations,
when wee made them,—& those proiecters, that should pro-
pound The advantage of them, for benefitt deserves to bee
whipte Through Every Parish in England,—& I know your
Majesties wisedome And goodness, will banish them your
Courte,—for itt is good parlements That muste fill your purse
sire when the other doth nothing but offend your people,
—Now sire with your Majesties favor, I will speake of The
greateste Error of state, that Ever was Comitted, in These two
Laste Raynes,—And that is, they Ever rewarded their Enemies, & neglected their friends, that this is an undeniable truth
so publick to the vew of all the world,—as some Devines Have
been Raysed for itt, though few, but abundance of Lawyeres,
noble men, & gentle men, this way, to make them noble men,
This was butt a weake polisey to take of Enemies, nay they
would say hee was a Shrode man, wee muste please him, reward him, make him a Lord, give him An office: but for a
freind, hee is an honeste man, give him nothing, heel doe us no
hurte,—sertenly this polesy, was Braught out of the Indies,
where they pray to the divell, & not To God, for they say Gods
a good man, & will doe no body hurte Therefore they will pray
& flatter the Divell, that may hurte them,—what man Almoste
hath been raysed these two Raynes, that did not apose the
king, & the state, nay they had no other way to rayse themselves they thought, & therefore They plyd itt, which was the
Ruine of our kingdome,—How many In king James his time,

many, butt in your Royall fathers time, many more I could
name, a great many that your Majestie knowes Nott, which was
before your time,—& I could name a great many, that your
Majestie doth know, Even by dozens, but I am Loth to offend,
for feare they might punish mee att your Counsell Table,
—This was so much practiced, as Henery Martin that Holly
Soule, sayd hee would bee the greateste man In England, with
the king, one Askte him how, hee Answered because hee
would doe him all the mischeefe hee Could,—but To see this
woefull false state maxim, for by this meanes, the Kinges In-
creased their Enemies, Infinitly, & abated their Freinds, for
ther was not rewardes for the Hopers, that All Lookt to bee
raysed by oposeing, & their declination of Their freindes,
were not able to helpe them, this made Parlements, so re-
frectary to his Majestie, Every one oposing Thinking to bee
raysed, their perticuler, when the poore Comon wealth, was
but a Cloke for their ambition, this heated & over Heated
Every parlemente, as much, if not more than Any thing Else,
—To make Enemies, & Distroy freindes, amoste Pernitius
maxim, & a false one as Ever was, in the world,—The remedy
is very Easey, reward your freindes sire, & punish your Enemies, & then you shall have many freindes, & few Enemies,
—nay you muste punish that they may feele itt,—And though
you give them their liberty, afterward, bee sure Though you
forgive them, Lett them not come to your courte, or Ever rayse
them, for can they once finde that hole in your Majesties Royall
Coates as they can offend you, & have no Hurte, your Clemencey shall bee playd on, & they will not Care how they offend
you,—but when they see they are—Punishte & sett by, & no
hopes of Riseing, but by serving of your Majestie, I dare say
they will take care how they offend, And as careful how to
Serve your Majestie,—nay they will Say there Is no Jesting
with this king, Doe you remember how Such A a man was
punisht, & never Came In ag en, and others, therefore, Itt
shall bee an Itum to mee, I assure you Sire & doe you, remember How such a one was rewarded, for serveing the king,
well then by the Grace of God, I will serve him, & Lett others
disserve him As they please, but I will nott,—This sire muste
bee both their discourses, & behavior, & thus your Majestie will
qualefye parlements, And your whole kingdome, so much, as
your people, will both bless you, And thank you for itt, —————

An other great Error, was to suffer the subiectes to dispute The kinges prorogative, in westeminster hall, & in parlements which was a moste dangerous & a pernitius thing, & not the leste Cause of our Late miseries, to Lett Every body see what the king may doe, & what hee may not doe, & nothing makes a king Cheaper, or pulls him downe more then this, for itt is an old Maxim, the king can doe no wrong, & it is moste true, for hee is A bove the Law, & so are all Goverments in the world, monarkey, Democresey, or Arestocresey, to Leve these Greeke wordes in Shorte, there is no Govermente, but it is Eyther by one or more, & still the trancsendant power, is to doe what itt Please, for it is Lefte to him, or more, to Judge the Laws, being trusted by the subiects, to that End, as prime Judge,-when they talke of the Lawe, the Lawyeres will make itt a measureing Caste on both sides, by their disputs & then whoe shall Judge it, Butt the supreame Judge,—Butt the suffering of these disputes, I Beleeve grew out of an opinion, that what soever a king would Have, devines Should make itt good by the lawes of God,—& the lawyeres Should make itt good, by the Lawes of the kingdome, itt is true, wise states some times makes use of both those professions, for their Endes, some-times, but Itt muste not bee with disputes, but declearations, or such thinges for disputes will make your Majestie goe much less, for your Majestie will take Care of disputes, by those persons, whose professions are to speak on both sides, which are Logitians & orators, devines, & Lawyeres, There fore lett your Majesties prorogative bee Ever held so sacred as never To bee disputed, for the moste dangerous Consequence that may follow, But God forbidd but the Subiecte may have sutes with the king, for Matter of Title, as for Land, or Leases, butt then that subiecte Muste aske the king leave firste, & then the king never denies Them,—An other Error in makeing so many Privey Counsellors, As they Could not fitt att the Table,—the old saying is two can keepe Counsell if one bee away, therefore the fewer the better,—Iff there bee use of the land soldeir your Majestie may have their opinions, And not need to make them privey Counsellors, so of sea men the Like, so of trade, lett the merchant deliver his opion, & not made A privey counsellore,—& so of the law, your Majestie May send for your Aturney, solister, & lerned Counsell of the Lawe, to Deliver their opinions, without makeing them privey Counsellors, Nay

my Lord Strafford was of opinion, to have no Lawyeres of
your privey Counsell, For they did but Distracte state affayres,—as I can tell your Majestie In Queen Elizabeths time,
old Burley, tolde her Majestie, that hee saw A Ruine Comeing
uppon her, for there was nothing almoste of state Affayeres,
that Came to the bord, but Edgerton that was Lord keeper,
Then, would Cross itt, with saying itt was againeste the Lawe,
& this In the Ende Sayes hee will bee your Majesties Ruine, so
they thought to Putt him outt, but at laste, sire Robert Cissill
the Lord Burleys son which was then Secretary, thought hee
had found a way how To helpte itt & itt was this to make
Poppam, then Lord Cheef Justice, a greate Lawyere, & hated
Edgerton, to make him A privey Counsellor, & so to poyse
Edgerton, & hee was made A privey Counsellor, & what soever
Edgerton sayd hee oposed it, And then they thought all was
well, butt within a few yeares, These two great Lawyeres,
agreed, & then they were worse Then Ever,—for Lawyeres
would Governe Armyes, by Ployden, Littletons tenures, & the
statutes, at large, & not by Martiall Lawe,—which would bee a
very fine Legall no Govermente of an Armey—Long orations
at Counsell one to Speake like Tulley, & the other like tasitus,
in very redicullous, & moste unfitt, for a Counsell table, To
heare themselves twatle away so much pretius time, to no
purpose, for a Counsellor should deliver his opinion as Cleare,
& as Shorte, as hee can, & to that purpose I think The Booke of
orders, for the Table Derectes it so,—for state Affayres, I
should wish your Majestie to Comunecate them to non Butt
your two Secretarys of state, & one more at the moste, & your
selfe to dispose of them,—————An other Error & a great
one they always suffered Parlements to Sitt to long, for when
They have presented their Grevanses, & Desires, & those—
Rectefied for the good of the Comon wealth, they should bee
dismiste, which is a great benefitt to the gentle men, to follow
Their owne affayres, as well as for your Majestie, for a parlemente will never wante worke, & what they have not, they will
make, as this laste did to the distraction, of our Antiente
kinges, To our setled Church & our old fundamentall,
Lawes—& The Inslaveing the whole nation,—therefore your
Majestie should Doe very well, to prefix them a time, how long
they should Sitt, & your Majestie & your people will finde
greate Ease In itt,—No Courtier that is not a privey Coun-

sellor, to medle with State affayres, butt your Majestie to Checke him & you will finde the Ease of itt,—nor no Groomes of the Bedd chamber, to make with Petitions, & busines, more then belongs to himselfe, for your Majestie hath masters of requestes, for all Petitions, & so Every man keepe within his owne Circle, of his office, & place, For I assure you sire their medleing did much disorder the Comon wealth, for their perticuler Gayne,—there is an other Error that doth over heate your people Extreamly And doth your Majestie much hurte, which is that Every man now Is becomed a state man, & itt is merly with the weekly Corants, Both att home & a broad, therefore they should bee forbid Eyther Domesticke or forayne news, as also such fellowes As Captin Rosingame, that made £500 a yeare with writting Newes to severall persons, this did as much hurte as the other if not more, for in a letter hee might bee bolder Then they Durste bee in printe this too, not only to bee For-biden absolutly butt to bee punisht, severly if they offend in this, kinde, this will so Coole the nation & quiett state speritts, as your Majestie & your subiects will finde greate Ease in itt,—so all our discourse will bee of Hunting & Hawkeing, Boling, Cocking, & such things, & bee Ever ready To serve your Majestie —————————————————
The Secretaryes of state heretofore did not very well, as Cooke,—& Vayne, for the £1500 per anum they had for intelegence They putt that upp in their owne purses & only gave the king Exchange newes from the merchants,—But I should humbly desire your Majestie not to Lett your Secretaryes wante for intellegence, And always Cherish them, & in rich them, for they Deserve Itt, for they have very much in their hands,—& sertenly sire Hee that hath moste & beste Intelegence, muste bee wiseste,—for sertenly hee that knowes moste, muste Bee wiseste, & that is Intelegence, therefore your Majestie Muste never starve your Instruments, for Intelegence, which are your Secretaryes, for your Embasadors, are to begg, & Publike for itt, but your Secretaries will finde you our many meane men, that will give you better, & they should—Always strive to make some Considerable person your Majesties By a good pention, both Counsellors in france, spayne, & Roome, & Jesuitts feede for the same purpose, whoe Confesses All maner of people, & knowes the greateste Secretts of state Intelegence sire Is the life of a state, & an Armey,

with Secresy And therefore nothing Should bee spared for Intelegence,—The Cardinall De Richlew was the wiseste & greateste statsman, In his time & hee went playnely to worke, without Litle—Juglings, hee had butt two thinges, which hee did all, with all, which was money & Armes, saying if the money would not doe, The Armes would, & if the Armes fayled, the money would, & if They were singley to weake, being Joyned they would Effecte moste thinges in this world, for their are very few above the price of money, & your Majestie sees what worke hee made in the world with itt, & one of our greateste Instruments of our Late troubles, & to that purpose hee desired the king of france That hee might have alwayes so many hundered thousande pistoles, Allways leying by him, which hee had,—And I assure your Majestie That the king of spayne hath done more with his money Then with his Armeys, oh sire Itt is powerfull both in church And Comon wealth, for itt makes popes & Cardinalls, & Intices Greate subiects from their Loyallty, as your Majestie well knowes, And therefore I beseech your Majestie bee rich, since you see what Benefitt would come to you, both att home & a broade by itt,

An other Error was, & a great one, to, that most officers were misplacet, for hee that is fitt to bee BBp of Canterbury Is not fitt to bee Generall, nor hee that is fitt to bee a generall, To bee Bishopp of Canterbury,—a Taylor to make shoes, & a Shoemaker, briches, this breeds a confution, & the king, & the Comonwealth ill served, this was so Comonly done as a merrry Mutition that I knowe, desired the place of the kinges bag-piper, which is £50 a yeare, one told him, hee wonderd hee would desire Itt, since hee knew nothing of itt, hee sayd therefore hee Hopte to have itt, for they always gave places, to those That were moste unfitt, for them, as a Luteneste place, to one that playd of the viole, & a violest place to one that Playd of the Lute,—And so in higher offices which was our bayne, As sir Henery Vayne to bee made Secretary, that could Hardly write & reade,—so to Anihilate the race of statesmen, As for Exsample In Queen Elizabeths dayes a gentle man would put his younger son, to the universety, then to the Ins of Courte, to have a smakering in the Lawe, afterwardes to wayte of an Embasador, afterwardes, to bee his secretary, Then to bee Lefte as Agente, or resedent, behind him, then sent of many

forrayne Imployments,—& after some 30 yeares Breeding, to
bee made a Clarke of the Signett, or a Clarke of the Counsell,—itt may bee afterwards, Secretary of state,—this was not
onely breeding, but a breed of statesmen, fitt to serve the
greateste monarke in the world,—Butt when great Favoritts
Came In, they Justled outt this Breed of stattesmen whoe soever would give a thousend pound more for the place, hee
Had itt, so the gentery seeing that, disposed of their sons
otherwise, as to the Gospell, the Lawe, & to bee merchants, &
so our race of statesmen, was at an End,—An other Error
Though Less, to put meane men into Serve your Majestie,
—prince Henery had men of a £1000 & £2000 a yeare, for his
Cupp bearers suers, & Carvers, not for the Pention of £20 a
yeare, but for the Honor to serve him,—these were men able
to serve you in the Countery, & Comon wealth, & would never
fayle your Majestie, when meane & begerly men can bee of no
use to your Majestie but A perpetuall charge, when the other
what soever your Majestie gives Then, you shall have something a gen still worth your money,—Prince Harry I have
heard had a note of all Excellent Persons, what soever in any
Arte, so to Draw them neere him, And to his Service, as occation still offered itt Selfe,—I Have heard Even to rare Locke
Smiths, hee hath had in His note,—this is a greate advantage to
princes, not only to bee well served, but bee knowing in Every
thing,—for a man, That hath studdyed £40 yeares, with great
Labor, & at Laste Hath found out some new & ingenious thing
in any Arte what advantage is itt to your Majestie to have him
deliver all This to you in halfe an Houer,—prince Harry was a
hope full Prince,—but truely sire without flattery, you much
Exceed Him, In all thinges in his owne way, & many, many,
thinges—that hee had not,—doth your Majestie Remember
Ingenious BBps And many more when your Majestie was
prince,—And now I will End this discourse with this, that, that
cannot Punish, & reward, In Juste time, cannot Governe, for
there Is no more to governe, this world, but by reward &
punishmente, & itt muste bee done in the very nicke of time,
orr Else Itt is to no purpose,—wee know no more that God
Almighty Hath but reward, & punishmente, both for this
world & the Nexte, in this world by afflictions, & bless-
inges,—& in the next world, his Heaven, & his Hell, which is
reward & punishmente, And your Majestie being Gods true

Anoynted & his Debuty uppon Earth, next & immediatly after christe, how can your Majestie follow A better presedent, which I know both your goodnes & wisedome will doe,—& the great God Ever prosper you, & preserve you.

Off The Courte Tables

Only a few wordes of your Majesties Tables, to your Severall officers, which I beleeve standes your Majestie In £40,000 a yeare, which is one of the greateste Honors, both to your Majesties courte And kingdome that I know,—neyther hath all the kinges in Christendome such tables, therefore itt were pitty they Should goe less, as many petty proiects, have been for itt, Butt itt is as true, that they should bee better ordered Then they have been, that your Majestie would bee pleased to Speake to your Lord stuard of your house hold, & to the Controller And Treasurer of your houshold,—that the Tables which your Majestie Alowes should all bee spent within the Courte, & not to bee caryed out to their perticuler houses, for their wifes, & Children, But all spent in your Majesties Courte, for the Honor of your Majesties Courte, & kingdome, so that all strangers, french, spanierds Etalians, Allmans, or any other may bee Invited to the Severall Tables, according to their Degrees, & qualeties, And so all other Lordes, knights, & gentle men, of worth That can serve your Majestie, In the Countery, when these waite of your Majestie, of a Sunday or a Hollyday, that they may bee according To their Degrees, & qualeties Invited to the Severall Tables, which gives a greate Satisfaction, & pleases them Infenitly,—so That your Majestie will bee pleased to give a stricte order that itt shall bee so, —which will please them moste of all, that your Majestie Takes such care of them,—And these Countery Lordes to carry the Sorde before your Majestie to the Chapell, in their turnes, they would Take itt as it is, for a great dell of Honor, & your Majesite to Speake To them sometimes, as they goe, & to thanke them for their Attendance, would Infenitly please & oblige them, for Litle Things many times produces great thinges, as great thinges sometimes produces Litle ones,—

For Your Majesties Devertisementes

Kinge James, & king Charles, your Majesties Royall father & Grand Father, alwayes aboute Michillmas went to Poyston, In Stable time, both for Hunting, & hawkeing, both at the feild & Att the River,—this would not only refresh your Majestie with the Sweat Ayre & wholesome Exersises, but unbende your more serious Thoughts, from the wayght of business, that you would have at London, though busines will follow your Majestie where soever you Are, but not such thronges of itt, this sire will mentayne—Health, & Long Life, better then Phisicke, which Long Life & Health, may they Ever attend you,—besides itt will bee such A refreshing to the Citie, when they have you agen, with such Joy, to see your Majestie, besides their Gayne,—well sire then your Majestie Is well returned to white hall, & there prepare a maske for Twelve tide,—Etalienes makes the Seanes beste, & all but your Majestie May have their Glorious Atier of Coper, which will Doe as well For two or three nightes, as silver, or Gold, & much Less charge, which otherwise will bee much found faulte withall, by those That attende your Majestie, in the maske,—I Should wish the firste time, That it is performed, to have all the Lordes, & their Ladyes, Sons, & Daughters, knights & gentle men, of qualety, & their Sons, & Daughters, Invited, to itt, & Every one to have ticketts From the Lord Chamberline for their Enterance, & the Lord Chamberline to bee very carefull, that none Else Enters, butt those that are Invited, to a voyd confution & Disorder, And the Lordes, & Ladyes, to bee Invited to Severall Tables, that Nighte, & the Lord chamberline to give order, to see them carefully Placet,—The second time itt is performed I should wish your Majestie Should Invite the Ins of courte, & non Else,—The Third time it was performed, I Should wish your Majestie Should Invite the Lord maior, Sheriffes, & all the Aldermen, with their wives, sons, & Daughters, with the principall merchants, & no other to come In, & some hansome Banquett at Every time, & your Majestie to Drinke their Wellcome which would Infenitly Please them,—Att other times, to have Severall balls & Invite The young Ladyes, & give them a banquett, & Drinke their welcome with thanks,—So Every weeke to have Playes, & Invite The Lordes & Ladyes to

them,————Then your Majestie to ride your Horses of manege, twice a weeke, which will Incourage Noble men, to Doe
the Like, to wayte of you,—& To make matches, with the
Noble men, So many of aside, to rune Att the Ringe, for a
supper, & a play, or Some Litle Juell, for—A prise, besides this
to bee in the Tilte Yeard publikely, & the Lordes And the
Ladeies to vew itt, & they also to bee Invited to this supper And
Play, —————————————————————————————
Then sire allwayes uppon your Coronation Day In Comem
oration of That blessed time, to have, a Tilting by your young
Lordes, & other Great persons, which I assure your Majestie is
the most Glorious Sight That can bee seen, & the most man-
lyeste,—though one Sayd, That Tilting was to Litle for Ear-
neste, & to much for Jeste, But this Tiltting will make your
Lordes good horse men, & to keepe Good horses,—They will
Dispute againeste itt for the Charge, That may Easeyly bee
Answered, Copper Lace will bee very Cheape, & will make as
good a show, for one Day as the beste,—all Queen Elizabeths
Dayes Shee had itt, & king James, & the king your Majesties
Father of blessed memory was the beste man at Armes, I vow
To God that Ever I saw, both for Grace & Surenes, Eyther at
Running at the Ring or runing at Tilte,—I dare not to advice
your Majestie to run at Tilte, because a king of france was kild
at Tilte, by the Earle of Mongomery, a strang acsedent, a
splinter stricking In at the sight of his Bevor,—but your Royall
father Run offten at Tilte, & thankes bee to God, never had
any Hurte,—And for Gameing Sertentimes your Majestie will
Sett downe As also, for Tenis, & Pall-malies Goffe, & other
recreations for winter, ——————————————————
St. Georges feaste Should bee kepte very strictly, but Every
knighte, to bee Limited, not to have above 50 men, a peece, for
otherwise the Charge would bee vaste, & hurte their Estates
very much, though not undoe them, —————————————

Itt may please your Majestie now Lente growes on, & I Should
wish your Majestie to goe to newe markett, which is the
Sweetest place in the world, & beste Ayre, & no place Like itt,
for Hunting, Hawkeing, And Courseing, & Horse Races, &
your Royall father Sayd hee did Alwayes furnish himselfe
there, with horses & houndes, for Sumer hunting,—And to
that purpose your Majestie will bee pleased To Invite the

northerne Lordes, & gentery, that hath the beste Horses & houndes, as also from the other partes,—Butt they muste Have long warning to provied leaste they make Excuses,—but Sertenly when it is knowne your Majestie will bee their, & the time, A greate store of the beste will wayte of you,—Itt is fleete hounds, Northerne houndes, that muste serve your Majestie, for a stagg will not bee kilde with Slow ones, in any time, & thus your Majestie will bee provieded & have your sportes, to Boote, ——————————————————————————

There is only one thing at new Markett that I wish mighte Bee mended, & that is there are So many High wayes together & Rutts, Made by a bundance of waggens, & Cartes, that comes That way, that when a sente lies Cross those wayes, it is Most Dangerous Riding, Indeed a horse at full speed, nay uppon A Gallopp, cannot posibley hold his feete but muste fall, as the Earle of hollande did over those wayes, most dangerously, & had much A Doe to recover itt, though hee had the best Phititans, & surgions That were at Courte, but this is Easeyly remedied sire for itt is butt Plowing them Even, & all is well, & no Danger at all, nor no Hinderance, for the waggoners, or waggens, Itt were well, if your Majestie Made Litle wagers with houndes, one againest an other, which beste For Sente, & vew, & then they muste bee markte with Severall Coullered Ribans,—or Else with Tarr, & oker, which are red and blacke that they may bee Distingishte, This putes Life in the huntsmen And masters, & heates them to greate mettle, whose Dogges Shall Conquer, that Day, & So Every Day that your Majestie Huntes ——————————————————————————

Your Majestie being at new Markett, you are So neare Cambridge, as the Chancelor, & the universety will Invite your Majestie thether, where They will most Royally Entertayne your Majestie, Every way besides Their orations, & Comodies, & Every Sunday Send your Majestie moste Excellent Prechers to new markett, —————————————————————

Now sire againeste Easter your Majestie will Come to London, to the Joy of your Citie, & the Ladyes that have wanted a Courte So long,—& There your Majestie will Entertayne your Selfe with Severall Delights, And hunting in your Majesties neere Forrestes, Chaces, & parkes, untill your Progress, which will then Draw on a pace,—And in your Majesties Prograse In

the Severall Counties, I knowe your Majestie will Doe all you
Can, to please your people, both greate & Smale,—& to
Cherish the Greate ones, that hath power in their Severall
Counties—& when your Majestie hath kilde a stagg, or a Brace
of Buckes, to Send Them to such Lordes, or powerfull men,
which will bee taken Infenitly well, nay rather if your Majestie
Send that venison to their Ladyes, Itt will bee taken much
better, for as Sir Edward Cooke Sayd, which knew itt to well,
that the night Crowe was powerfull, & Indeed For the most
parte in England, the Gray mare is the better horse,—which I
profess & acknowledg, for my perticular, for truly I am Not
pleased Excepte itt bee so,—& when your Majestie Is happy In
A vertious Queen, I beleeve wee muste flatter her to, & good
Reson,—The meaner Sorte of Courtiers are very Peremtory
For the most parte, & gives the Country many times Juste
Cause To Complayne, & then I Should wish your Majestie, to
Satisfie the People, rather then a meane, Insolente Courtier
for Such Foolish meane officers Doth your Majestie Great
DisService,—

The Devertisements For Your Majesties People, both in the Citie, & Country

Firste for London, Paris Garden will Hold good for the
meaner People, ————————————————————————————
Then for Severall play HouSes, as there were five, at Leaste In
my time,—Blacke friers, the Cocke Pitt, SalSbury Courte, The
fortune, & the Redd Bull,—there were the boyes that playd At
black friers, & Paules, & then the kinges, players, playd at The
Globe, which is now Calde the Phenix,—Some playd at the
Bores heade, & at the Curtine in the Feildes, & Some at the
Hope, which is the Bare Garden, & Some at white friers,—but
five or Six playe houses is Enough, for all Sortes of peoples—
Devertion, & pleasure, in that kinde,—Then Pupett playes
Their will bee to please them besides,—as also Dancers of the
Ropes with Juglers, & Tumblers,—besides strange Sightes of
Beastes, birdes, monsters, & many other things; with Severall

Sorts of Musicke & Danceing, & all the old Hollydays, with
Their mirth, & rightes Sett upp agen, feasteing Dayly will bee,
In merry England, for England is So plentifull of all provition,
That iff wee Doe not Eate them, they will Eate us, So wee
Feaste, in our owne Defence, ———————————————

For the Country recreations

May Games, Moris Dances, the Lord of the may, & Lady of
the May, the Foole, & the Hoby Horse, muste not bee for-
gotten,—also the whitson Lord, & Lady,—Thrashing of
Henns, at Shrove tide—Carroles & wassells, at Christmas, with
good plum Porege & Pyes, which nowe Are forbiden, as pro-
phane, ungodly thinges,—wakes, fayeres, & Marketts, mentaynes Comerse, & trade,—& after Evening prayer Every
Sunday, & Hollyday, the Country people, with their—Fresher
Lasses, to tripp on the Towne Greane, a boute the may pole,
To the Lowder Bagg pipe, there to bee refreshte with their
Ale, & Cakes, king James of blessed memory, writt a litle
booke, not only in Defence of Danceing, but Comanded that
his good people Should reioyce themselfes, with Danceing
after Evening Prayer, Then there Should bee players, to gow
upp, & Downe, the Country, In my time moste Noble-men had
Country players, Dancers on the Ropes, Juglers, Tumblers, &
indeed moste of all those thinges, I Formerly Spoke of, Comes
Downe into the Country,—& these things will much Diverte, &
please the People,—butt Mr. Thomas kilagree your Majesties
master of the Revells, I know will manege all those things
Moste Discretly, for your Majesties Honor,—& the good of the
Comon wealth, Lookeing leaste after his owne perticuller, or
Else I am much Mistaken,—These Devertismentes will amuse
the peoples thoughts And keepe them in harmless actions,
which will free your Majestie from Faction, & Rebellion.

For the Govermente of Scottland

Scottland is an Antient kingdome, full of Nobilety, & gentery, butt Their Lawes are quite Differente from ours,—And they would bee Loth to Change them, & Alterations for the most parte, is dangerous, And therefore I Should wish your Majestie to keep them, as they are, For itt will not bee worth the paynes, & trouble to Alter them,—For the Goverment of their Church I beleeve they are wearry of this, they have,—& will Petition your Majestie hereafter for Bishops Agen, butt truely untill they Petition your Majestie I would Lett them Alone In their owne way,—Then to Governe itt as it is now By an Armey I Should nott advise your Majestie to Doe So,—for the charge Is to greate, for any benefitt can Come to your Majestie of itt, firste Itt Discontents all your Subiectes, there,—& as long as your Majestie hath A Garison in barwicke, Carlile, Newcastle, & Tinmouth, I Dare Say, the Counties Trent north, will always Secuer your Majestie From Scottland, & no Danger, Excepte the two king domes Should A gree, agen, which I beleeve they will never Doe, So I Should-Humbley advice your Majestie to governe Scottland by their owne Lawes, And to bee governed by their owne Nation, Such as your Majestie Shall thinke fitt to opoynte both for the Sivell & Miletarye Govermente, the strong places to bee in Such hands as may bee Faythfull if itt bee posible,—There are many Gallant persons in This kingdome, but being not so rich, your Majestie will bee pleased to bee kinde to them,—for I assure your Majestie Queen Elizabeth, with A very litle money, did governe Scottland more absolutely, then anye kinge, or Queen of itt, Ever Did,—butt I thinke itt is growne Deerer Now,—they are apt to bee factious, & great anymoseties, one Againeste an other, in their owne Country, though not out of itt, which your Majestie Continually, may make your Advantage off,—to all the Secretts of Scottland,—And where Scottland did Depend uppon france, heeretofore, when the kingdomes were Separated, As Scottland when they were opreste by England, to have Suckers, & helpe from france, & so when the English made warr In france, then the Scotts to Deverte that warr, to make warrs in England, butt itt Served Eyther of their turnes, so Litle, as Edward the third, that Galland kinge, & his son that unpareled brave blacke prince, calde so because of his blacke Armor, that hee wore, I Say this brave kinge, & gallant prince In the famous Batle, of Poytiers,—tooke the king of france prisoner And at the Same time, those Lordes the king lefte behind him, took The king of Scotts prisoner, & both these kinges, mett prisoners Att winsor Castle,—butt for the relation that Scottland hath Now to france, is no great matter, for though they have the Privelige of the nation, if they have not much money, to bye land, Leases, houses, or offices, itt Signefieth Litle, or nothing,—And what is it to the Scotch nation, for one man to have—A troope off horse, or for a few to holde halbertes, & to bee of the king of france his Garde, nothing, therefore they Looke To have their Shares of the Sweet of England, & therefore will Depend uppon your Majestie & for the king of france, Since Scottland Is Joyned to England, hee Doth not much valew them, since now They cannot Serve his turne, —though ther are some Litle affections of the Scotts remayneing to the french, but they are but weake, & the affections of the french weaker to them,—but so Long as your Majestie is master of England, there is no feare of Scottland, there is no man in the world knowes both the kingdome & the people better then your Majestie doth, which is a great blessing for Scottland, & much a greater blessing for England.

For the Govermente off Irelande

Your Majestie knowes well that Ireland is A Subordinate kingdome To England, governed by the Same Lawes, & your Majestie will bee pleased That they may have good Lawyeres, & Juste Judges, which they Have not Ever been happy In, the kingdome is very fertill, And plentifull, of all provitions, but by reson the people are Naturally Lasey, the kingdome is not husbanded & Cultivated As it aught to bee, tis true, it is poor but that is not the Faulte of the kingdome, but merly wante of trade, which trade Makes Every kingdome, Rich—& Sertenly no kingdome, is Better Seated for trade, then Ireland, haveing the beste partes And Havens in the world, & sertenly had the Earle of Strafford Continued there, any time, hee had made

that kingdome by Trade, & Increasing their Shipping very
rich & himself nott The poorer for itt,—And thus have
braught your Majestie greate reveneus out of Ireland, which
heretofore was alwayes a very greate Charge, To the kingdome of England, but I have heard Some Say, that A Parlemente In England would bee againeste the Inriching of Ireland, Thinkeing itt would bee a preiudice to England, by
takeing of so Much of the Trade a way in England, but I have
heard no Solide Arguments for itt, & untill I doe I Should
thinke your Majestie had Better have two rich kingdomes then
one,—for England would Bee Shrodly put to itt, to mentayne
two kingdomes, more then itt Selfe, & so your Majesties Coffers might bee Emty your Majesties Royall Predesesers had
always, a good Armey in Ireland, & I Should alwayes wish your
Majestie So to have, rather to Increase itt, then to Deminishe
Itt, not only for the Safety & quiett of the Subiectes there, butt
uppon Any occation that is nesesary, your Majestie might
transporte the For your Service,-A wise Juste & Honorable
person for your Lord—Leuftenante there,—Is very nesesary,
—& truely I know none So fitt as the Lord Marquis of ormond,
or Deserves it like him, or can Serve your Majestie halfe so well,
being able, & knowing in That kingdome, Loyall, faythfull to
your Seriuce, & affectionat To your Majestie person,—The
Irish are naturally Lasey, & apte to Bee sturd, to Rebellion by
their Prestes, whoe have greete power over them,—as the
french king had power over the Scotts, So the king of Spayne
had to great an Intreste in Ireland, wittnes the Earle of Ter-
one,—for that Rebellion Did emty Queen Elizabeths Coffers,
—as I was told old Burley Sayd,—that helpeing Henery the
forth of france, Setting upp the states of the Low Counterys
—Pulling Downe the king of Spayne, by her warr with him So
poore As hee was beggd for in Churches, & absolutly Governing Scottland, And with all this, Sayes old Burley, yett my
misteris Sayde hee had money In her Coffers, but hee vowed if
the warr with Ireland held but a litle longer, that the Queen
would bee the Arantes begger, of any king or Queen in the
Christian world,—The king of Spayne made warr by way of
Devertion, Hee was So Tormented with the English warr,
—And now sire Give mee Leave to tell you this Story, king
James of blesed Memory Cald for the Lord Chichester, whoe
had been many yeares Debuty of Ireland, & a very wise man, &

Comanded him to tell Him truely the Dispotitions & humores
of his Irish Subiectes The Natives which were the old Irish, &
hee Answered, if it Please your Majestie I will tell you the truth
In shorte,—they Are a very Scurvey People, & they have been
as Scurveyly used, For the firste, I know not, butt for the Laste
I Dare Sweare, Is true, & I thinke there are a greate many
wittnesses for itt, Both English & Scotts, that knowes it full
well, & have Gayned well by itt, & the meaneste people &
bankeroutes wente thether, & within a few yeares, grew to
Huge Riches, And to bee Great Lordes, so your Majestie Sees
what a frutfull Place your kingdome of Ireland Is, —————

For Govermente In Generall

There hath been a greate question for kinges, wether they
Should Governe, by Love, or feare, many Arguments for
Love, but one,—if the people Love him, there is nothing that
Hee can desire, that the Subiecte will not grante, & it is with
that Ease, pleasure, & sweetnes, as nothing can bee—Better,
but those that are for governing by feare, Say Shrewdly, they
Say, that Love Depends of them, & not of The king, & that
their Love is various, & Alterable upoon Every, & no occation,—But with feare Say they Dependes uppon the king, &
therefore that is the Sureste & Safeste way, Say they,—now
may it please your Majestie I am of neyther of Their
mindes,—butt I Should wish your Majestie to Governe by
Both, Love, & feare, mixte together as occation Serves,—
Haveing the power which is force, & never to use it but uppon
Nesesety, when there is Eyther Comotion, or to prevente Itt,
when any what soever begins to Sow Sedition, between The
king & his people, & to Governe as god Almighty Doth By
promises, & threatings, rewardes for Doeing well, & Punish-
ments, for those that offende —————
Then the great studdy & learning for kinges & wise men Is not
to reade bookes, but to reade men, for all business in The
world is in men,—wittneses, are in men, Jueries are men
Judges are men, greate officers are men,—favoritts, are men,

And Greate monarkes, kinges, & princes, are men,—Nay that
which is So Sublime Devinety, is Governed by men, as the
convocations, of Bishops In England are men,—the Classis are
men, the pope And the Cardinalls are men,—& though they
Say the pope is chosen By the holly Goste, if it were So I dare
Say the french kinge And king of spayne, would offer him a
bribe on Eyther Side To gett the pope of the Spanish Side, or
on the french Side, & all the Cardinalls are perpetually De-
vieded between france & spayne by Bribes,—All Devine
Counsells which are Devine parlements Are men, & pacte
Counsells, Comonly, wittnes the Counsell of Trente,—all
statesmen, are men, all parlements, are men,—So that hee that
is a master of reading of men, knowing Their Dispotitions, &
which Baite is moste proper to hooke Them withall, Gaynes his
business, in all kindes, for the Lawe is A nose of wax, & is to bee
puld any way as those men pleaseth, And for Counsell on both
Sides makes itt a measureing Caste, So that the Judge may
Judge itt, of which Side hee pleaseth, & heth Lawe for itt,—nay
the Holly writt how itt is Disputed on all Sides, Juste Contrary
on to the other, & both aledges Textes, for itt, Nay the Same
texte pro & con,—there are three hundereth Severall opinions, on this smale texte, This is my Body, So That in their
Severall kingdomes, men Judge itt, & wee muste obey their
Judgmentes, wether itt bee right or wrong, Because it standes
for right or wrong,—Because it standes for righte, as long as
that Authorety Hath power to Judge itt,—So that Gayne, the
men & all is gained, So that Sertenly the wiseste studdy, is to
read men, since all Thinges in this world Lies in their
Handes, ————————————————————————
Education is a mighty matter,—they call itt a Second nature,
but I beleeve it is converted into nature, & is nature itt Selfe,
for Iff wee Consider nature, no more, then weeping, Laugh-
ing, hungrey, Thurstey, Eateing, drinking, urenising, & the
Sege, &c,—but very These, are altered perpetually by Custome, but all the reste is very Custome,—for though a man had
never So Excellent an Naturall witt, borne with him, what is
that naturall witt when hee is borne no more, but his five sences
cleere to Bring outward obiectes to his brayne, & his brayne of
such A temper, as to dispose well of them, when they are there,
So that if this Excellente mother witt had no obiectes that
Came In, but hee kepte in a Dungion, untill hee were twenty

Yeares old,—& then bring him out, hee would bee Less knowing Then a well Educated Dogg, because his braynes hath had nothing to worke of, but when it hath then the naturall witt, Shews it Selfe, & Custome, is the great Tirante of man kinde, Doth it not for the most parte make men of such Religions, As they are of, & Consience, both by Custome of breeding, Else why Should it bee againeste a protestantes Contience, to goe To mass, & a papistes Contience, to goe to our prayers, but by Custome of breeding, I will not Speake of knaves that Alters their Religon, or opinions for gayne, or an unsetled Foole, but what for the most parte Governes the world, for wee are not to make an Exseption a Rule, for there is no Rule, without an Exseption & Sertenly were a Childe Educated In Turkey, hee would bee a turke, & give god thankes for itt, As wee Doe the Contrary, how Should hee Doe otherwise,—for St Paule Sayeth, that fayth Comes by heareing, where are there Fircer turkes, then the Janesaries, which are Christians Childeren, So powerfull sire Is Custome, it is converted into nature, & is Nature, & In the bloud, as for Exsample, a Soldeire is Sicke of A fevor, & hee tells his Doctor, what an ill night hee hath had, with troublesome Dreames, that hee Dreamte hee was to make a bridg, good, & how his Leggs, & Armes, were shott of, And tumbled into the watter, & all his men Loste, what is this butt Custome, A Sealious brother, that hath our bookes of Marters, by harte, with offten reading, when hee is in a fevor Complaynes to his Doctor of troublesome Dreames, that hee was Condemnde to Dye, for his Religion, to bee burnte in Smithfeild, But that in the mideste of the flames, hee found such comforte Singing the 25th Salme, & his Soule assended to heaven in that Fiery charriott,—what is this but custome,—nay a Litle child Dreames, how Jacke a Dandy followed him, & frighted him, custome Nay Custome is so Powerfull, as a Philosopher told mee, that A Barr of Iron, in a window standing there, 30 yeares, though The Endes were Equally poysed yett that End that used to bee, dounewards, will tend dounwards, if it bee put in a Dish, & That Dish in watter, & if Custome have Such power of Iron, what Should it have of flesh, & bloud,—oh it is powerfull, Nay it is as powerfull when one is a wake, & well as in sichnes And a Sleepe, —but indeed all our lives is but wakeing Dreames, As for Exsample, a man that hath been Piously Educated Sees Some-

thing that is white, when Soever wee See that wee Are always simulising, as white as snow, white as a Lilly or Something, So this Godly Educated man, Sees white presently hee thinkes, white as a Sirplis, that Sirplis upon A preacher, that preacher in a pulpett, preaching on the Passion, presently hee strickes his breste, & is at his prayers, with holly Eiachulations,—this is custome,—An other that hath been bred more in Cavelleir, when hee Sees white hee is Simulising itt, to as white as a Smocke That smocke uppon a beautyfull venus, Loves Sayles Hoyste upp, for Qupids voyage, & hee Inbarked, floting on loves Tossing weaves, what is this but Custome,—nay it is so powerfull, as wee Argue, it, thinking, wee chuse the beste by our Excellent Judgmente, when custome absolutly Swayes us, as for Exsample, your Majestie knowes some Lordes That are alwayes Golloping upp & Downe, being persuaded still, itt is the best for them, though they are often Deceaved in it, yett still they are at it agen,—& merly Transported by Custome, —Another gentleman, which is A most faythfull & affectionat Servant to your Majestie of my knowledge, whoe hath had a long Custome of Lasines And hee fortefies himselfe, as hee thinkes, with many Excellent Arguments, to Sett still, when it is not his Arguments But the Longe Custome of Lasines, that Swayes his Arguments, Yett I beseech your Majestie give mee Leave to Say Somethinge in The behalfe of that gentleman, first hee hath much a doe To live & sitt still, therefore hee hath no moneys for Jurneys, nexte hee hath been very sickly of late, &, Lastly hee is growne old, all which three things I Dare Answere for him, hee is very Sorry for, & these three thinges were Enough to keepe him at home without Custome, So I have Answered as well as I can for my freind, for truely I have found very few Else, a freind to him, —————————————
As a naturall good witt in a Dungion is nothing without Education, In Seeing the Greate world, & Considering of itt, So is Education, Less without haveing a good witt, for Itt makes him but the more foole, for Coriatt could Speake Greeke & stand on his Head, & yett hee was butt An Ase, An Artifitiall foole, oh witt flyes a bove all Thinges in the world a high pitch, for that which they call Learneing puts a good witt out of the right way of knowledge, with false Artes,—for what is the Arte of poetry, the Arte, of Logicke, & the Arte of Retoricke, nothing but the Imetation of nature, & farr Shorte of her to, for

Horace his Arte of poetry will never make a good Poett, if hee bee not so by nature, nor Aristotles Logicke with his premises, & conclutions, make a wise states man, if hee bee not so by nature, nor Aristotles retorick Make a good orator, if hee bee not So by nature,—I have heard the Bishops of Salisbury Say, which was an Excellent orator, that the Arte of Retorick did never helpe him, but his owne, Naturall witt,—no it is not Eufania Gratia, will doe Any good, if hee have not a good naturall witt of his owne,—For when nature gave any one the Gifte of Poetery, Logick, Retoricke, naturally, then Some Laborious dull fellow, tooke Notes of what they Sayd, & put it into a method & that Method they Call the Artes of those three,—A good memorey, A good witt, which is Simulizing of wordes, & thinges, & a good Judgment, which is rightly to Distinguish, & all those naturally with Education, In great Cities, at home, & a broad, In Severall Courtes, & in Severall Armyes is beyond all the Educations In all the uniuerseties, in the world, a man that Hath a good witt, that hath Converste withall Sortes of People, from the begger to the king,—such witts are borne To Lead, & not to follow, to teach & not to Learne,—but There are but few of them,—Sir Walter Rawley was one of them, & some one or two, more & those were all that Ever I knew in all my Time,—And now sire I beseech you Majestie to forgive this Philosophicall Digression, for I could not helpe itt, because it came in my way,—but to Conclud with what I began withall, they that would seeme to bee So much for the king, as to forgett the Comon wealth, doth the king very great Disservece, & they that Seeme to bee of so much for the Comon wealth, as to forgett the king doth The Comon wealth worse Service,—for Sertenly the king, & the Comonwealth is no more to bee Separated Then Christe & his Church.

For Forayne States

Iff Please your Majestie I will begin firste, with the states of the Low Counterys, as conserning your Majesties Intereste moste,—when your Majestie Is well Settled, in your throne, & hath money in your purse, Then I would humbley advice your

Majestie to Demand of the states the Same priveleges, Queen Elizabeth had, which is to have—Flushing, & the Brill, in your Majesties handes, & a Garison of your owne in them; some may Say they may take them a way, when they will, itt is true, but they Dare not for feare your Majestie Should make a warr, with them, & if your Majestie had, Had those two Townes, now in your handes, they would have been of great use to you, the nexte is that your Majesties Embasador Should Sitt in all their Counsells, as they Did in Queen Elizabeths time,—the nexte is So many foote & horse always To asiste you, as also Such number of Shipping, your Majestie Paying for them,—To pay your Majestie a rente for their Herring Fishing—& your Majestie also to fish, for there is Enough for Both, & then a Leage offensive and defensive with them, for Holland muste bee your Majesties out worke, & thus your Majestie need not Care for all the Christian world, for it is the Sea, that will over Awe all your great neyghbores, but Some will say what if they will not Doe itt, then your Majestie may beate Them to itt, with great fasilety, & barr them your portes, And they are undone, & therefore itt is in your Majesties power, And not in theirs, & therefore Sertenly your Majestie Cannot doe Better, then to Doe itt,—but your Majestie will bee care full not to bee Diswaded from that which will bee So advantagious To you, for Sertenly sire they will offer to brib all your great officers, which they have done alwayes, & So have gott Their Endes,—but your Majestie will Soone finde out that by their Arguments, though they handle it never so cuningly,—with saying It is a moste dangerous thing, at this time considering the coniuncture of afayres, very formerly, when tis their worshipps bribes,

For France & Spayne

When your Majestie is well Setled in your Throne, & all your kingdomes In obedience, & peace & your Majestie good Sumes in your purse, Then I Should humbley advice your Majestie to have a warr with one of these great kinges,—To begin with france I Should thinke better for alwayes the nearest neyghbores Are the moste trouble some, Espetially

being So powerfull, The Animosety hath been Long, & great
between the two Nations, the English, & the french, for when
Soever in story the french, names the Enemy without any
other adition Hee meanes alwayes the English, That warr then
that your Majestie makes with the french, I would not have itt
by Land by no meanes,—for when your Majesties Royall An-
cesters Made a warr in france, then there was a Duke of
Britaney, Normandy, Burgandy, Lorayne, & many other
petty princes which tooke parte with England, & now moste of
these are added to the Crowne of france, & some Devided
otherwayes which makes a greate Difference, In makeing a
warr by Land Therefore the Advantagious warr your Majestie
is to make with France, is to bee made by Sea,—so that your
Majestie may burne all his Shipps In his Havens, & not Suffer a
french shipp To stay any where, butt Eyther to take him or
Sincke him, & this continued butt a few yeares, will bring him
to reson In rich your Majesties kingdome, Impoverish his, &
make him Nothing by Sea att all which now is growne to strong
which is Dangerous for your kingdome & this will Secuer you
where you need not feare an Invation, for hee will have no
Shipping to Transporte them, & besides wether the king of
Spayne bee in warr, or peace, with the French hee will un-
derhand give your Majestie good Sums yearly, Both to make &
Continue the warr with the french,—when your Majestie hath
pared the king of frances nayles thus by sea Then harken to a
peace with him, which your Majestie may have uppon your
owne Conditions,—And then have a warr with spayne And by
Sea, to which the french will give your Majestie good Sums
yearely for to make that warr, & to continue itt, for Lewis the
Eleventh the Craftiest fox that Ever was king of france, for
feare of Edward the forth, Gave him at An enterwew in france
a great Sum of money And So yearely to with draw his Armey,
& to have a peace, And the story Sayes I thinke, it was Comines,
that a french Lord Speakeing of the Agreement, Sayd that
Pention that My king gives yours, you are mistaken, Sayes the
English Lord, it is a tribute,—but for the warr with spayne, to
Asalte his Indies, I doe not like, the Spanard is So well Fortefied, & so strong there, & the voyag is So long that our men
would bee So weake, as they would nott bee fitt To fighte,—I
know not what the Barbadoes, the Barmodoes virgina, New
England, & new Scotland might helpe, Butt I Doubte butt Litle

yett,—therefore the warr Should Bee by Sea, butt no Invation,—to hinder his trade, to hinder His Silver flote, & that
would begger him in a litle time, As Queen Elizabeth Did, &
your Majestie will bee three times as Strong, by Sea, as shee
was,—for the reste of the prince, they Are So petty ones, as I
will not trouble your Majestie with Speakeing of them, for all
the rest are Devided between france & Spayne, ———————
The advantages of A forren warr & with these two kinges in
their turnes Are first they will bee So weakend, as your Majestie needes Nott feare them for any invation,—Then itt will
In rich your Majesties kingdome very much Increase your
Majesties Shipping—busie your people, & the looser Sorte, as
also the better Sorte to bee full of Imploymente, vent the
over-plus, that would bee a burthen to the kingdome, make
your people—warrlike, & Espetially by Sea, which is your
Majesties greatest Strength, for makeing a forren warr, keepes
your Majestie Safe at home, both from Invation, & Sivill
warr—when a Softe & Long peace, makes a Civill warr, fo-
mented By Devines, & Lawyeres, for the people must bee
busied with Something, or Else they will finde worke themselves, though to the Ruine of the kingdome, therefore There
is nothing Like a forren warr, for your Majesties Safety, And
Honor, for the good of your people & kingdomes,—And So
the Greate God Ever Bless, Prosper, & Preserve you,———

Index*

* The index was prepared by Rande S. Aaronson and financed by a grant from the Rutgers University Research Council